NON-TRADITIONAL METHODS OF BUYING REAL ESTATE

AN INVALUABLE GUIDE FOR ANYONE WISHING TO PURCHASE TAX SALE PROPERTY

 TSP PUBLICATIONS

Canadian Cataloguing in Publication Data

Gordon, Paul
 Non-traditional methods of buying real estate : an invaluable guide for anyone wishing to purchase tax sale property.

 Includes sections on purchasing property through sheriffs' sales, real estate auctions, provincial crown land, foreclosures and power of sale, federal surplus land, etc . . .

 ISBN 0-9695031-0-5

 1. Real estate investment.   I. Title.

 HD1379.G67 1991   332.63'24   C91-090030-2

TSP PUBLICATIONS
P.O. BOX 5380
STATION F, OTTAWA
CANADA, K2C 3J1

Printed and bound in Canada

The following publication – which is based on the personal experiences of the author – is intended to help the reader quickly understand little-known methods of acquiring real estate.

This book is sold with the understanding that neither the author nor the publisher is engaged in rendering legal or real estate services. Questions relevant to the practice of law or real estate should be addressed to a member of those professions.

The author and publisher specifically disclaim any liability, loss, or risk, personal or otherwise, which is incurred as a consequence, directly or indirectly, of the use and application of any of the contents of this work.

CONTENTS

LIST OF SAMPLES AND ILLUSTRATIONS ix

INTRODUCTION 1

CHAPTER ONE   Understanding Tax Sales

1   An Overview... 7
2   Why Properties Are Sold for Tax Arrears 10
3   Where Are the Properties Located............................ 10
4   How Properties Are Advertised.............................. 11
5   How to Find Out Where and When Tax Sales Will Be Held 16
6   Municipal Tax Sale Rules.................................... 19
7   Taking Possession.. 24
8   Tax Registration Procedure.................................. 25

CHAPTER TWO   Doing Your Own Search

9   Consulting an Historical Atlas............................... 30
10   Acquiring a Good County Map 33
11   Investing in a Few Good Topographical Maps............... 34
12   Air Photography.. 42
13   How to Tell if You Have Enough Information 46
14   Land Titles and Registry Offices 47
15   Using Registry Offices...................................... 49
16   Using Land Titles Offices 53
17   Using the Assessment Department 57
18   Canadian Almanac and Directory........................... 58

CHAPTER THREE   Seeing the Property and Getting Ready for the Sale

19   Now to See the Actual Piece of Property 63
20   Estimating the Value of the Property 64
21   Do I Get Clear Title? 68
22   Public Auctions... 69

CHAPTER FOUR   Buying Country Property

23   Checking the Dwelling 75
24   Water... 78
25   Electricity... 80
26   Sewage System 81
27   Soil Content 82
28   Working the Soil 85
29   Zoning... 86
30   Land Severance.. 91
31   Other Factors to Consider... 93
32   Improving Your Purchase for Resale 96
33   Using a Real Estate Agent 100
34   Mortgages 102
35   Waterfront Property 105

CHAPTER FIVE   A Close Look at Tax Sale Procedures in Each Province

36   Tax Sale Procedures in Each Province..........................113

CHAPTER SIX   Other Non-Traditional Methods of Acquiring Real Estate

37   Sheriffs' Sales of Land 139
38   Surplus Federal Crown Property 142
39   Real Estate Auctions...145
40   Crown Land 148
41   Foreclosure and Power of Sale 149
42   An Alternative Approach...151

CHAPTER SEVEN Frequently Asked Questions 153

APPENDICES

A Tax Sale Checklist 161

B Addresses of Provincial Gazettes Which Publish
   Notices of Tax Sales 163

C Mapping and Aerial Photography for Provinces
   and Jurisdictions 164

D Tax Arrears Certificate 165

E Imperial-Metric Conversion Tables 166

F Ontario Land Registry Offices 167

G Glossary 169

LIST OF SAMPLES AND ILLUSTRATIONS

Title	Page
# 1 Sale by Public Auction	13
# 2 Form 8 (Tender to Purchase)	22
# 3 Map From Historical Atlas	31
# 4 Sample of Scales	35
# 5 Topographical Map Symbols	36
# 6 Road Symbols on Topographical Maps	37
# 7 Illustration of a Hill and its Contours	38
# 8 Illustration of Imaginary Hill Rising From Sea Level	39
# 9 Illustration of a Pocket Stereoscope	43
#10 Placement of Stereoscope in Order to View Two Overlapping Photos	43
#11 Page From an Abstract Book	51
#12 Surveyor's Description	55
#13 R-Plan	56
#14 Page from The Canadian Almanac and Directory	60
#15 Types of Zones	87
#16 Sale by Public Tender	115
#17 Listing From Gazette officielle du Québec	117
#18 Tax Sale for the City of Montreal	118
#19 Advertisement for a City of Vancouver Tax Sale	121
#20 Organized Territory Tax Sale Notice	123
#21 Listing from The Alberta Gazette	125
#22 Listing from The Manitoba Gazette	126
#23 Tax Lien	128
#24 Newspaper Advertisement of a Saskatchewan Tax Sale	128

#25   Partial Listing From a Nova Scotia Municipal
      Tax Sale Notice..130
#26   Listing From the Royal Gazette.....................132
#27   Newfoundland Notice of Tax Sale................135
#28   P.E.I. Royal Gazette Tax Sale Notices..........136
#29   Newspaper Advertisement for Sheriff's Sale 140
#30   Newspaper Advertisement of Real Estate Auction 146
#31   Newspaper Advertisement for Power of Sale.............151

Introduction

Most people in our society are looking for financial security. Many have found that security by purchasing real estate. Why real estate? Probably because buying property is one of the safest investments you can make: stocks can go bust, gold and silver values can fluctuate, but real estate will appreciate, provide an edge against inflation, and serve as leverage for the purchase of other properties. Unfortunately, there is a limited amount of land out there, and we all want a piece of it to call our own.

Usually, real estate transactions result from the listing of a property with a real estate agent or from "For Sale by Owner" opportunities. We refer to these as traditional approaches to buying real estate. Little known to much of the public, however, are several other methods of buying property, methods that frequently allow the purchaser to acquire a piece of real estate for much less than market value. **Non-Traditional Methods of Buying Real Estate** (A Guide to Buying Tax Sale Property) is written for those who are interested in discovering these other possibilities.

This book is designed first, to give a comprehensive view and thorough understanding of purchasing property through tax sales and secondly, to familiarize the reader with other non-traditional methods of acquiring real estate.

While tax sales are used as the primary example throughout much of the book, most of what is written in regards to these sales is applicable to all types of real estate transactions.

1

Chapter one takes a close look at properties being sold because of non-payment of taxes. It gives a description of the tax sale procedure, an explanation as to why properties are sold for tax arrears, how they are listed, and how to find out where and when these sales are held. It outlines the municipal rules governing these sales and gives a summary of what takes place if you are the successful purchaser.

Chapter two is the working chapter. It makes you aware of several sources that can help you learn more about properties sold for tax arrears: geographical, topographical, and aerial photo maps, the Canadian Almanac and Directory, and the Registry and Land Titles Offices.

Chapter three shows you how to estimate the value of a property, discusses the question of clear title, and looks closely at the auction process.

Chapter four focuses on the important points to consider when buying country or waterfront property, since many of the properties sold at tax sales are in rural areas.

Chapter five takes an in-depth look at tax sale procedures in all ten provinces. Included are examples of the types of tax sale notices used to advertise upcoming sales.

Chapter six examines other non-traditional property buying opportunities such as sheriffs' sales, surplus federal Crown property, real estate auctions, Crown land opportunities, foreclosures, and power of sale.

Chapter seven gives answers to the most frequently asked questions dealing with tax sales.

As a further aid to the reader, the writer includes definitions to many of the real estate terms encountered throughout the book, as well as illustrations, addresses and sample forms for clarification.

To conclude, it is the author's belief that there is no easy way to make a fortune in real estate, but being aware of all the options certainly increases your chances of doing so. We hope that after reading **Non-Traditional Methods of Buying Real Estate** you will have a more complete picture of the exciting world of Canadian real estate.

Chapter
One

Understanding Tax Sales

An Overview

A tax sale can be defined as the selling of a property by tax authorities when the owner of the property has failed to meet a tax liability. The sale is usually by public auction, but it may be arranged by tender or sealed bids. Usually, the purchaser acquires immediate title and possession of the property offered for sale. Occasionally, the purchaser's right to possession of the property is postponed in order to enable the delinquent taxpayer a specified period of time in which to repay the tax.

The proceeds of the sale are used to pay the unpaid tax and other expenses that were incurred in listing the property. The balance, if any, is usually paid to the delinquent taxpayer.

In some cases, when taxes due on a property remain unpaid, the tax authority may sell, at public auction, a "lien" obtained against the delinquent taxpayer's property. The successful bidder can subsequently convert this lien into ownership of the property if the sums due are not paid by the delinquent taxpayer within a specified redemption period.

Tax sales occur in every province of Canada. However, the disposition of these properties varies because municipal and provincial acts governing these sales differ from province to province.

The following section gives a brief summary of tax sale procedures used by municipal and provincial authorities. Chapter 5 examines each province in more detail and gives samples of tax sale notices.

Steps Leading to a Tax Sale

Where any part of a municipality's property taxes are outstanding after a two year period, the municipal treasurer may prepare a *tax arrears certificate* and register it in the appropriate Registry or Land Titles Office. For example, 1988 taxes that remain unpaid to December 31st 1990, would be subject to registration on January 1st, 1991.

The *tax arrears certificate* (for one provincial example, see Form 2 in the Appendix) must contain an accurate description of the land. In addition, there must be an indication that the land described will be sold by public sale if the *cancellation price* is not paid to the municipality within one year of the registration of the tax arrears certificate. By *cancellation price*, we refer to an amount equal to all tax arrears owing, penalties and interests, and all reasonable costs incurred by the municipality as a result of this procedure. Included in the costs are legal fees and disbursements, the costs of a survey, and advertising expenses.

The treasurer is required to send or cause to be sent, within sixty (60) days of the registration of a tax arrears certificate, a notice to the owner and all interested parties, advising them of the registration and potential sale of the property.

Included in those who receive notice are the assessed tenants in occupation of the land and their spouses. Where a notice has been sent to the owner of the land, a separate notice must also be addressed to his/her spouse.

A person is not entitled to a notice if the treasurer does not find his/her address after having completed a reasonable search of the records of the Registry Office, the Land Titles Office, the Sheriff's Office, and the last returned assessment roll.

After sending the proper notices, the treasurer must prepare and register, in the appropriate Land Titles or Registry Office, a statutory declaration stating the names and addresses of the people to whom notices have been sent.

By law, any person can pay the cancellation price to the municipality, but it must be done within one year from the day on which the tax arrears certificate was registered. When such a payment is received, the treasurer must register a *tax arrears cancellation certificate*. Once this certificate is registered, the process is halted. The person who pays the cancellation price before the end of the one year period may request that the treasurer prepare an itemized breakdown of the cancellation price. The request must be in writing and made within thirty (30) days of the payment.

Legislation in some provinces gives permission to a municipality to enter into an agreement with the owner of the land which allows for extending the time in which a tax arrear payment must be made. This agreement may set out such things as the number and amount of each installment required to be paid, but it cannot reduce the cancellation price nor prohibit any person from paying the cancellation price at any time.

In the event that the cancellation price still remains unpaid 280 days after the day of registration of the tax arrears certificate, the treasurer will be required to send a final notice. This notice is sent to the same parties who received the initial notice and again warns of the pending sale if the cancellation price is not paid before the expiry of the one year redemption period.

If the cancellation price continues to be unpaid, the treasurer must advertise that the property will be sold. Once advertised, these properties can be disposed of either by public auction or by public tender. The sales are always subject to certain rules and follow procedures which have been established by provincial regulations (see Section 6 for Municipal Tax Sale Rules). At these sales, the minimum acceptable offer on a property is always the cancellation price.

A municipality may, if the council authorizes it, bid or tender on a property being offered for sale. The municipality must, however, have a municipal purpose for the property.

Why Properties Are Sold for Tax Arrears

T he reasons are varied and numerous, but some of the most common seem to be any one, or combination, of the following: active dissent among joint property holders, none of whom are willing to take legal action to resolve their diverse claims; death of the owner without having a will; financial misfortune with ensuing oppressive judgements being levied against the property; the owner being a resident in some foreign country and totally unaware of the actual value of the property in question, etc.... Whatever the reason or reasons, if you own real estate and fail to pay your municipal taxes, your property will inevitably end up in the hands of the authorities.

Where Are the Properties Located?

T o begin, one must realize that Canada is a vast country. Consequently, you will find that listings cover many areas, some of which will be very close to your home town and some which will be found several hundred miles away.

In a one year period, properties advertised will cover different parts of each province. The properties are of many types, from farms, houses, cottages, and bush lots, to islands and business locations. They vary from small lots to parcels which are hundreds of acres in size.

Upcoming sales are listed only when the treasurer decides that it is time for a sale to take place. These decisions are made at different times, thus allowing sales to take place in different areas throughout the year.

In your hunt for a tax sale property, do not restrict yourself to one specific area. Explore various areas. The experience gained will prove well worthwhile.

4

How Properties Are Advertised

A ll tax sale listings are advertised in a similar manner. Notification of sale consists of a legal description and, at times, will also include an address and the name of the assessed owner(s). Descriptions of these properties tend to be quite brief and often require contacting the municipality holding the sale in order to learn more about each property. (See Sample 1-1 for an advertisement which was placed in a provincial gazette and also appeared for four consecutive weeks in a major local newspaper servicing that municipality.)

In Chapter 5 we have given samples of tax sale listings for all ten Canadian provinces. As you study the various methods of advertising tax arrear properties, it will become apparent that slight variations occur between provinces.

You will notice in Sample 1-1 that notification is given regarding the time and place of the public auction. Next comes a legal description of the lands which are to be sold, along with a dollar figure representing the minimum amount at which bidding can occur. A statement indicates that the successful purchaser must pay in full, at the time of the sale, the amount of the successful bid. This is usually paid by cash, money order, or by bank draft or cheque certified by a bank or trust company. A brief comment follows regarding the municipality's responsibility and a statement is made regarding what statutes and rules are governing the sale. Finally,the name of the contact person is given in the event that further information is required

In most provinces, tax sales are held by public auction. Some provinces, such as Ontario, have the option of holding their sales either by public tender or public auction.

While tax sale advertisements give a mailing address in the event that further information is required, they seldom, if ever, give the telephone number of the municipal office in question. It is quite possible that the number is available in your telephone directory or through the information service of your telephone company. However, in our research, we have uncovered a publication entitled the Canadian Almanac and Directory (published every year) which lists the telephone numbers of all villages, townships, towns, regional municipalities, cities, etc. . . . For every municipality, it provides the mailing address, the population total, the county or district in which it is located, and the name of the municipal clerk or treasurer.

The Almanac contains a wealth of information useful for anyone who decides to get involved in tax sales. Section 18 of this book gives more details on the value of the Canadian Almanac and Directory.

Sale of Land for Tax Arrears by Public Auction

Municipal Tax Sales Act

The Corporation of the County of Hastings

Take notice that land(s) described below will be offered for sale by Public Auction at 10:00 o'clock in the forenoon on the 26th day of January, 1989, at the County of Hastings Administration Building, 235 Pinnacle Street, Belleville, Ontario.

Parcel Number	Description of Land	Minimum Bid
1.	Township of Sidney, County of Hastings, Lot 29, Plan 1124, being part Lot 15, Broken Front..	$4,458.94
2.	Township of Sidney, County of Hastings, Parcel 430-1 Section 21 D-2, being part of Lot 5, Concession 2	$1,519.62
3.	Township of Sidney, County of Hastings, Lot 1, Plan 227, in the Village of Tupperville, being part of Lot 9, Concession 8.............	$ 815.92
4.	Township of Rawdon, County of Hastings, Lot 12, Plan M-39, being part of Lot 23, Concession 13	$ 656.03
5.	Township of Huntington, County of Hastings, being part of Lot 13, Concession 3, as follows: Premising that the westerly limit of said Lot 13, has a bearing of north 19° 19' west derived from Reference Plan 21R-755 and relating all bearings herein thereto: Commencing at the southwest corner of said Lot 13; Thence north 19° 19' west a distance of 95.75 feet to a point being the point of commencement; Thence north 52° 54' east a distance of 109.04 feet to an iron bar planted; Thence continuing north 52° 54' east a distance of 88.75 feet to an iron bar planted; Thence north 4° 54' west a distance of 103.49 feet to an iron bar planted; Thence northwesterly on a curve to the left having a radius of 231.48 feet, an arc distance of 92.45 feet (the chord equivalent being 91.84 feet measured north 57° 46'20" west) to an iron bar planted: Thence north 69° 13' west a distance of 58.78 feet to an iron bar planted; Thence south 77° 22' 30" west 112.79 feet more or less along an existing fence to a point in the westerly limit of said Lot 13, Concession 3; Thence southerly along the westerly limit of said Lot 13 a distance of 283.56 feet more or less to the point of commencement. This description is the same description contained in Deed number 208200	$ 933.47
6.	Township of Huntingdon, County of Hastings, Parts 8 and 9, Reference Plan 21R2694, being part of Lot 7, Concession 13	$1,091.80
7.	Township of Marmora, County of Hastings, Part 3, Plan 21R 2164, being part of Lot 8, Concession 3. This description is the same description contained in Deed number 306147	$ 726.49
8.	Township of Marmora, County of Hastings, Lot 72, Plan M-72, together with a 1/162 interest in Blocks 16 and 18 Plan M-70, Block 59, 61, 62, 63, 64 Plan M-71 and Blocks 92, 93, 94, 95, 96, 97, 98, 99, and 100, 101, and 102. Plan M-72, being part Lot 3, Concession 4	$ 851.48

13

9. Township of Lake, County of Hastings, Part of Lot 78, West of the Hastings Road, described as follows: Composed of Lot 78, west of the Hastings Road, Excepting thereout and therefrom that part thereof heretofore conveyed, described as follows: Commencing at the point where the northerly limit of said Lot 78 meets the westerly limit of said Hastings Road; Thence in southerly direction along the westerly limit of said road a distance of 250' to a point (being at the southeasterly angle of the land conveyed to Morin); Thence westerly in a straight line parallel with the northerly limit of said Lot 78 to a point in the westerly limit of said Lot; Thence northerly along said westerly limit of said Lot, 250' to the northwest angle of said Lot; Thence easterly along said northerly limit of said Lot to a place of beginning. This description is the same description contained in Deed number 14684.. $ 775.39

10. Township of Madoc, County of Hastings, Plan 155 in the village of Bannockburn, Lot 2 and 3, Saving and Excepting thereout and therefrom the Highway described according to Plan 854 and Plan 883.. $ 565.58

11. Township of Tudor, County of Hastings, being the north half of the south half of Lot 10, Concession 4, containing 23.5 acres ..... $ 811.01

12. Township of Wollaston, County of Hastings, Part of Lot 20, Concession 14, described as follows: Bounded on the north by a line drawn parallel to the northerly boundary of the said Lot at a distance of 2640 feet therefrom, on the east by the easterly boundary of the said Lot, on the south by a line drawn parallel to the northerly boundary of the said Lot at a distance of 2,970 feet therefrom, and on the west by the westerly boundary of the said Lot, containing 10 acres...................................... $ 655.82

13. Township of Limerick, County of Hastings, Part of Lot 17, Concession 3, described as follows: Bounded on the east by the easterly limit of said Lot; Bounded on the south by a line drawn parallel to the southerly limit of the said Lot and distant therefrom 1760 feet. This description is the same description contained in Deed number 59440 .... $ 883.42

14. Township of Faraday, County of Hastings, Lot 30, Registrar's Compiled Plan 2310, in Lot 9, Concession 10............................ $1,959.79

15. Township of Faraday, County of Hastings, Lot 22, Registrar's Compiled Plan 2321, being part of Lot 9, Concession A .... $ 483.56

16. Township of Dungannon, County of Hastings, Lot 16, Registrar's Compiled Plan 1929, being part of Lots 9 and 10, Concession 7, part H.S.R. Plan 284, Part 16................................ $ 700.91

17. Township of Wicklow, County of Hastings, Part of Lot 31, Concession 1, described as follows: Firstly – Starting at a post on the eastern boundary of said Lot 31 where Highway Number 62 intersects said Lot 31 and running west along the southerly boundary of said Highway a distance of 370 feet; Thence north 115 feet to the point of commencement; Thence west 70 feet; Thence north 75 feet; Thence east 70 feet; Thence south 75 feet to the point of commencement. Secondly – Starting at a post on

the easterly boundary of said Lot 31 where Highway Number 62 intersects said Lot and running west along the northern boundary of said Highway a distance of 370 feet; Thence north 190 feet to the point of commencement. Thence on north 75 feet; Thence west 70 feet; Thence south 75 feet; Thence east 70 feet to the point of commencement. This description is the same description contained in Deed number 83877 .... $1,523.62

All amounts payable by the successful purchaser shall be payable in full at the time of the sale by cash or money order or by bank draft or cheque certified by a bank, trust company or Province of Ontario Savings Office.

The municipality makes no representation regarding the title to or any other matters relating to the land to be sold. Responsibility for ascertaining these matters rests with the potential purchasers.

This sale is governed by the Municipal Tax Sales Act, 1984, and the Municipal Tax Sales Rules. The successful purchaser will be required to pay the amount bid plus accumulated taxes and the relevant land transfer tax.

For further information regarding this sale contact:

> D.A.Smart
> Deputy Treasurer
> The Corporation of the County of Hastings,
> 235 Pinnacle Street,
> Postal Bag 4400,
> County Administration Building,
> Belleville, Ontario, K1N 3A9.

Copies of the Canadian Almanac and Directory are generally kept in your local library. They can also be purchased from the following source.

> Canadian Almanac and Directory
> 2775 Matheson Blvd.
> Mississauga, Ontario
> L4W 4P7

The Canadian Almanac and Directory is also carried by some bookstores. However, because it is an expensive publication, you may need to call several bookstores before finding one that carries this large book.

When looking at the advertisement section entitled "Description of Lands", the obvious comes to mind. How can you tell what the property actually looks like from the type of description given? *Don't panic.* In almost every sale you will

15

find municipal officials most cooperative. In fact, they almost always make a point of preparing some sort of documentation on each property. Municipal officials can give you the directions needed to locate the property and often, they will even provide you with a good map. Information packages are usually mailed upon request and they will help you locate the property more easily.

Some municipalities have a mailing list. For a nominal fee, authorities will send you an information package on upcoming tax sales.

If you receive little or no information from the municipality holding the sale, you may require further guidance on how to do your own search of the property. (See Chapter 2, Doing Your Own Search.)

5
How to Find Out Where and When Tax Sales Will Be Held

T here are 3 ways of obtaining specific details about upcoming tax sales.

The best source of information for sales in your area is the community newspaper. Without exception, all ten provinces require that municipalities advertise any upcoming tax sales in at least one widely circulated newspaper of that municipality. They often appear once a week, for several weeks, prior to the sale. Though not always the case, they often appear in the *Legal*

Notices section of the paper. There should be a period of at least 7 days after the publication of the last advertisement in the newspaper and the holding of an actual tax sale.

One drawback to this source is that you will only learn of the tax sales taking place in your immediate area. Sales occurring in other parts of the province will be advertised in the newspapers of those areas. For most people, this is more than acceptable.

If no local newspaper exists, the properties for sale must be posted in the municipal office and one other prominent place in the municipality.

The second source of information is the official gazette published by each province.The value of this source is that it will inform you of all sales held throughout the province. While gazettes are published by all ten provincial governments, it must be pointed out that tax sale notices only appear in the following provincial gazettes.

Ontario
Quebec
British Columbia
Alberta
Manitoba
New Brunswick
Prince Edward Island

Provincial gazettes are usually published weekly and tax sale listings can appear in any of the 52 issues. You can quickly determine whether an issue contains a notice of tax sale by consulting the index. If a sale is listed, you will usually see headings such as "Notice of Tax Sale", "Sale of Lands for Arrears of Taxes", or "Public Sale of Land".

Subscriptions to provincial gazettes can be quite costly. Nevertheless, if your province lists all sales in the gazette, it is the most accurate source of information regarding upcoming tax sales.

In the Appendix, you will find the address for each provincial gazette listing tax arrear properties. For more information about single issues and/or subscription costs, you are advised to write to the addresses given.

PLEASE NOTE: Provincial gazettes can be consulted free of charge at most public libraries. However, in some cases, the most recent issues of the gazette are put on the shelf only a few days before the actual date of the sale, or even after the sale has already taken place. Before eliminating your library as an excellent source of information, you should ask your librarian or check your library's gazette collection to see how quickly the issues are made available. If having access to the most recent issues is a problem, perhaps expressing your concern is all that is required in order to have free tax sale information at your fingertips.

The last source where information can be obtained is by calling directly the local town, village, township, or municipality of your area and asking the clerk or treasurer if and when they are planning to hold a tax sale. It is important to remember that sales are not held every year and that, for smaller municipalities, sales may in fact be several years apart. Telephone numbers for these should be available in your local telephone directory or through the telephone information service. Another source of municipal telephone numbers, addresses, and names of clerks or treasurers is a publication entitled the CANADIAN ALMANAC and DIRECTORY (see Section 18 for address).

## 6

Municipal Tax Sale Rules

A s previously mentioned, all ten provinces have specific guidelines and procedures which they must follow when holding a sale of tax arrear properties. Certain elements are common to each province, but variations do occur. Consequently, the following description of municipal tax sale rules cannot be too specific. In instances where numbers are given (Ex: 3 weeks, 20%, 7 days, 3.00 p.m. etc. . .) it is important to realize that there will be slight differences for each province.

Sales by Public Auction

- For most provinces, the property must be advertised as least once in the provincial gazette.

- The sale must be advertised for 4 consecutive weeks in a widely circulated newspaper(s) of that municipality. There should be a period of at least 7 days after the publication of the last advertisement in the newspaper before holding of the auction.

- The place, date, and time of the auction are to be clearly specified in the advertisements.

- The treasurer or his designate must act as auctioneer.

- For each parcel of land to be sold during the auction, the auctioneer must

  - in opening or reopening the bidding on the parcel, state the minimum bid as set out in the advertisement

  - acknowledge each bidder, repeat each bid made, and call for higher bids

- if no higher bid is made, repeat the last bid three times and if there is still no higher bid, acknowledge the highest bidder.

- The highest bidder will be declared to be the successful purchaser if the bidder immediately pays the amount bid, the applicable land transfer tax, and the accumulated taxes, in cash (money order, bank draft or certified cheque) to the auctioneer.

- If the highest bidder fails to make the payment, the auctioneer shall forthwith reopen the bidding.

- If no bid is made for a parcel of land or there is no successful purchaser, the property will be taken over by the municipality.

- The auctioneer will issue a receipt to the successful purchaser for the amount received and the receipt will include a legal description of the parcel of land, the name of the purchaser, and the date in which the tax deed will be registered.

- The auctioneer will declare the auction closed upon completion of the bidding on all the parcels of land offered for sale at the auction.

Sales by Public Tender

- For most provinces the sale must be advertised at least once in the provincial gazette.

- The sale must be advertised for 4 consecutive weeks in a widely circulated newspaper(s) of that municipality. There should be a period of at least 7 days after the publication of the last advertisement in the newspaper whereby tenders can be submitted.

- Tenders are usually obtained from the municipal office and often follow the format of Form 8 (see Sample 1-2).

- The municipality must always specify the minimum tender required, this being the amount of back taxes due and expenses incurred.

- If one wishes to submit a tender, it must be accompanied by a deposit of at least 20 per cent of the tender amount. Because this 20 per cent is your deposit, it should be made by way of money order, bank draft, or cheque certified by a bank or trust company.

- The tender, along with the required form, is to be submitted in a sealed envelope on the outside of which is indicated "Tax Sale for   " (give a short description or municipal address of the property sufficient to permit the treasurer to identify the parcel of land to which the tender relates). Insert your sealed tender into a second envelope and address it to the treasurer. The address of the latter is always given in the Gazette or newspaper advertisement.

- A tender can relate to only one parcel of land. Separate tenders are required if you wish to bid on more than one property.

- On receiving an envelope identified as containing a tender, the treasurer will mark on it the time and date of its receipt and will retain it unopened in a safe place.

- When two or more tenders are for equal amounts, (if this should occur) the tender that was received earlier will be deemed to be higher.

- A tender is withdrawn if the tenderer's written request to have the tender withdrawn is received by the treasurer before 3 p.m. local time on the last date for receiving tenders.

- The treasurer, at a place in the municipality that is open to the public, will open the sealed envelopes containing the tenders as soon as possible after 3 p.m. local time on the last date for receiving tenders.

- The sealed envelopes will be opened in the presence of at least one person who did not submit a tender, which person may be a municipal employee.

- After opening the sealed envelopes, the treasurer will examine their contents and reject every tender that

Sample 1-2   Form 8

Form 8
Tender to Purchase
Municipal Tax Sales Act, 1984

To: Name: _____

    Address:

    Telephone:

Re: Sale Of: (description of land)

1. I/we hereby tender to purchase the land described above for the amount of $_____
   (_____ dollars in accor-
   dance with the terms and conditions of the Municipal Tax Sales Act, 1984 and the Municipal
   Tax Sales Rules

2. I/we understand that this tender must be received by the Treasurer's Office not later that 3:00
   p.m. local time on
   _____ 19_____, and that in the event of this tender being accepted. I/we shall be notified of its acceptance.

3. I/we enclose a deposit in the form of a certified cheque/bank draft/money order for the sum of $_____
   (_____dollars) in the favour of the _____
                                               Name of the Municipality or Board
   representing 20 per cent or more of the tendered amount which will be forfeited if I/we are
   successful tenderers and I/we do not pay the balance of the tendered amount, any land
   transfer tax and any accumulated taxes within fourteen calendar days of the treasurer noti-
   fying me/us that I/we are the highest tenderer.

This tender is submitted pursuant to the *Municipal Tax Sales Tax Act, 1984* and the Municipal Tax
Sales Rules.

Dated at_____this_____day of _____ 19____ .

Name of Tenderer	Name of Tenderer
Address of Tenderer	Address of Tenderer

22

- is not equal to or greater than the minimum tender amount as shown in the advertisement

- does not have at least a 20 per cent deposit of the tender amount in the form of a money order, bank draft, or certified cheque

- does not come in a sealed envelope with the required information on it (See rule 6)

- includes any term or provision not provided for in these rules

- has been withdrawn (See rule 10).

- Afterwards, the treasurer will reject all but the two highest of the remaining tenders.

- Every rejected tender will be returned to the tenderer with the deposit, if any, and a statement giving the reason for rejection.

- If there is no tender, or successful tenderer, the treasurer will declare that this is the case and the property in question becomes a possession of the municipality.

- If there are two tenders remaining for a piece of property, the treasurer will notify the higher tenderer by ordinary mail sent to the address showing in the tender, that he/she will be declared to be the successful purchaser if, within fourteen calendar days of the mailing of notice, the balance of the amount tendered, the applicable land transfer tax, and the accumulated taxes are paid, in cash, to the treasurer.

- If the higher tenderer makes the payment, the treasurer will declare the tenderer to be the successful purchaser.

- If the higher tenderer does not make the payment, the tenderer's deposit will be forfeited forthwith to the municipality and the treasurer will offer the parcel to the second highest tenderer.

Taking Possession

All tenders on a property are opened at the same time. All rejected tenders are returned to tenderers. If the successful bidder fails to complete the purchase within the specified time period, the deposit will be lost and the property will be offered to the next highest bidder.

The successful purchaser at a tax sale (auction or tender), is notified and the treasurer prepares and registers a tax deed in the given name or in the name requested. The deed is final and binding when registered. A registered tax deed vests that the land is free and clear of all interests, except those of the Crown and of any easements or restrictive covenants that may have been previously attached to the land.

In some provinces, the successful bidder or tenderer is required to wait for a period of time before obtaining title to the property – usually one year. This is known as a "redemption period". In order for redemption to occur, the assessed owner must pay all outstanding taxes, all costs incurred by the tax collector, and, often, an interest charge on the money put forth at the tax sale by the successful bidder or tenderer. Upon the expiry of the redemption period, the successful bidder or tenderer receives clear title to the property. (Chapter 5 outlines which provinces have a redemption period.)

In the event that there is no successful purchaser at a tax sale, the municipality receives title to the property and the treasurer registers a notice of vesting in the name of the municipality. The municipality can then dispose of the property as it pleases. Most often, it is put on the market through a real estate company and is sold at market value.

Provincial Acts outline how the proceeds of a sale must be distributed. The money must be applied first, towards paying all of the cancellation price, secondly, to any person other than the owner who has an interest in the land, according to his/her priority at law, and finally, to the former owner.

While the Acts refer to *municipal tax sales,* it is possible for other tiers of government to hold tax sales. In order to do so, they must enter into an agreement, through by-law, with the local or area municipality. With the approval of the municipality(ies), a county, metropolitan or regional council can have its treasurer perform the duties of the municipal treasurer and thus also hold a tax sale.

8
Tax Registration Procedure

W hile there are many cities, townships, and counties that use tax sales in order to dispose of tax delinquent properties, it is important to stress that there are also many others that use a system called the "Tax Registration Procedure". (This term may vary depending on the province.) With the Tax Registration Procedure, the municipality notifies the property owner that the taxes are in arrears and that these taxes must be paid if he/she wishes to retain possession of the property. If, despite all attempts to secure payment of the back taxes, these still remain outstanding, the property is then usually taken over by the authorities in question. It is not offered for tenders nor is it auctioned. Instead it is sold at market value, used for rental purposes, or perhaps even converted into a park. The type of land determines its use.

If you are unsure as to what is done for your area, contact your city, municipality or county office to get an answer.

## Chapter Two

Doing Your Own Search

Doing Your Own Search

O nce you have discovered that a municipality is holding a tax sale, you will want to learn more about the various properties being sold. Many municipalities will send a comprehensive package giving further details about each property. For example, what you might receive is information specifying the size of the parcel and whether or not there are buildings on the land. The authorities will often also provide a map pinpointing the location of each property.

At other times, the municipality will provide nothing more than the legal description found in the notice of sale. If such is the case, the potential purchaser will have to depend on his/her own resources to find specific data on the property of interest.

Even when an information package is provided, it never answers all the questions that must be addressed in order to make a well thought-out purchase.

This chapter is designed to guide your efforts and help you acquire a clear picture of the parcel in question before you submit a tender or bid at an auction.

## 9

Consulting an Historical Atlas

(FOR PROVINCES USING THE LOTS AND CONCESSIONS SYSTEM TO DESCRIBE LAND DIVISIONS)

I f your province uses a system of lots and concessions (Ex: Ontario) in advertising tax arrear properties, provincial Historical Atlases can help you determine some of the characteristics of the property in question. Telephone your area Land Titles or Registry Office and ask if they use the lots and concessions system. If they do, you might visit your public library, bringing your tax sale listings, papers, and pen.

Let us assume that a sale is to take place in DRUMMOND TOWNSHIP. Find a librarian and tell him/her what county Drummond township is in, and request the Historical Atlas for the County of (in this case it is Lanark County). An atlas exists for every one of the older counties and once you know where to find these atlases you will not need to ask for directions again.

Let us continue with the above example. You now have the Historical Atlas for the County of Lanark. Flip through the pages until you locate the map for Drummond Township. Interestingly, you will find a map of this township as it was in approximately 1880 (see Sample 2-1, Map from Historical Atlas). Although newer roads and some landmarks may not be shown, the lots and concessions will be unchanged. If you are looking for Lot 14, Conc. 7, you can identify it in no time at all. In our sample map, a local town hall is on Lot 14, Conc.7. By

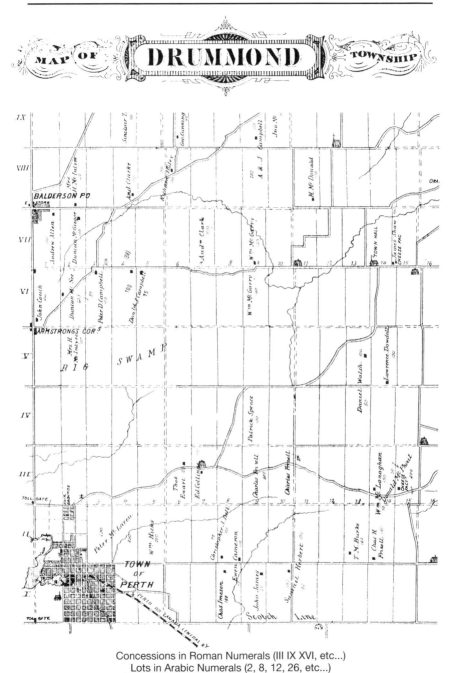

Concessions in Roman Numerals (III IX XVI, etc...)
Lots in Arabic Numerals (2, 8, 12, 26, etc...)

referring to Sample 2-1, you will see how the system of lots and concessions can be used to describe tax arrear properties.

If you are looking for waterfront land only, you can quickly see if any part of Lot 14, Conc. 7 is on a lake or river. If it isn't, you can dismiss it and look for another property on the listing.

If you are not especially interested in acquiring waterfront property, you will want to retain the information you have just found.

Make a little sketch of that part of the township map or get a photocopy of the page from the atlas. You could do the same for every listing in every township shown on the list. If you are just looking for waterfront property, you can rapidly eliminate properties where the map shows dry land only.

Do not hastily rule out a property just because the information is limited. Such a property could end up being an excellent buy. Check it out first, then you can make a decision as to whether it should be rejected or pursued.

Acquiring a Good County Map

(FOR PROVINCES USING THE LOTS AND CONCESSIONS SYSTEM)

While your sketch or photocopy from the Historical Atlas had value, it was used primarily as an early screening technique. You should acquire an up to date copy of the county maps for the area you are interested in so that you can better pinpoint the property. For example, if Drummond Township is of interest, acquiring the most recent map for Lanark County would be very helpful.

You can obtain county maps from two sources. One source is the County Clerk of the county in question. You will find the address and telephone number of each county clerk (and/or treasurer) in the CANADIAN ALMANAC and DIRECTORY which can be consulted at your public library (see Section 18). The county clerk should be able to send you a very large *white print* map of the county in question. For very large counties you may require as many as four map sections in order to have every township in the county.

Maps for every county in Ontario can also be obtained from The Map Office. Information on descriptions and prices can be obtained from the following address:

The Map Office
Ministry of Transportation and Communications
1201 Wilson Ave.
Downsview, Ont., M3M 1J8

Investing in a Few Good Topographical Maps

T opographical maps are very useful in determining the location and physical characteristics of any property. The following information will help you become a skilled reader of such maps.

A topographical map is a representation of the features of a portion of the surface of the earth drawn to scale on paper. The features shown are classified into four main divisions: WATER (including the sea, lakes, rivers, streams, ponds, marshes, and swamps), RELIEF (including mountains, hills, valleys, cliffs, slopes, and depths), CULTURE (including the works of man such as cities, towns, villages, buildings, railways, and land boundaries), and VEGETATION (including wooded areas, orchards, vineyards, and cleared areas). All of the above are represented through various symbols.

Once the scale of the map is known, distances can be quickly calculated, areas can be determined, and the true size of lakes, farms, villages, and towns can be measured. The scale of a map is usually given in one or more of three ways.

– A scale statement: 1 cm equals 2.5 km

– A scale ratio: 1:250,000

– A scale bar (see Figure 2-1, Illustration of scales.)

To a large extent the scale determines what features will appear on a map. For example, individual buildings are not shown on maps at 1:500,000 scale or smaller. On 1:250,000 scale maps, buildings are shown only if they constitute out-standing landmarks. At 1:50,000 all dwellings are shown,

Figure 2-1 Sample of Scales

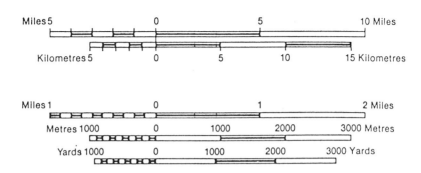

Scale 1:250,000
1 Inch to 4 Miles Approximately

except in the built-up areas of cities and towns where the whole developed area is tinted pink. At this scale, however, outbuildings such as garages and tool sheds are not shown. These appear at 1:20,000 scale, as do fences and landmark trees. At 1:2000 and larger scales, porches are shown on buildings, as well as features such as mailboxes and fire hydrants. The same general concept holds for water features: small ponds and backyard swimming pools appear only on large-scale maps.

Topographical maps use a system of symbols to identify landmarks and place them in their proper position. Symbols are designed to take very little space on the map. As well, they are drawn so as to resemble the feature represented. For example, a church is depicted by a small square building surmounted by a cross. Schools are indicated by the building symbol carrying a small flag. (See Figure 2-2, Topographical Map Symbols.)

Map symbols are of three types: point symbols, line symbols, and area symbols. Point symbols show the exact position of a feature that occupies a very small area. Included in this type are buildings, towers, wind pumps, bridges, wells, springs, dams, and swimming pools.

35

Figure 2-2 Some Topographical Map Symbols

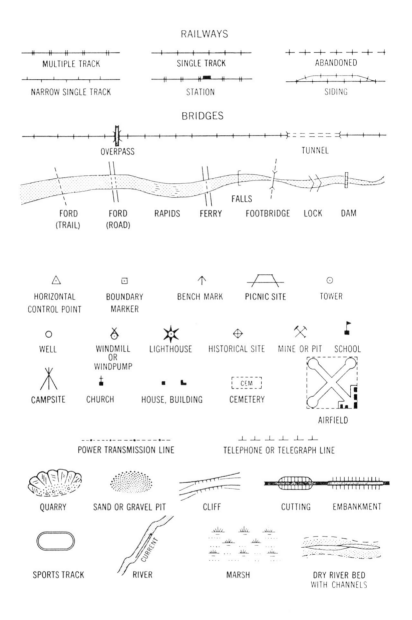

RAILWAYS

MULTIPLE TRACK   SINGLE TRACK   ABANDONED

NARROW SINGLE TRACK   STATION   SIDING

BRIDGES

OVERPASS   TUNNEL

FORD   FORD   RAPIDS   FERRY   FOOTBRIDGE   LOCK   DAM
(TRAIL) (ROAD)   FALLS

HORIZONTAL   BOUNDARY   BENCH MARK   PICNIC SITE   TOWER
CONTROL POINT   MARKER

WELL   WINDMILL   LIGHTHOUSE   HISTORICAL SITE   MINE OR PIT   SCHOOL
         OR
       WINDPUMP

CAMPSITE   CHURCH   HOUSE, BUILDING   CEMETERY

AIRFIELD

POWER TRANSMISSION LINE   TELEPHONE OR TELEGRAPH LINE

QUARRY   SAND OR GRAVEL PIT   CLIFF   CUTTING   EMBANKMENT

SPORTS TRACK   RIVER   MARSH   DRY RIVER BED
                          WITH CHANNELS

36

Figure 2-2   continued

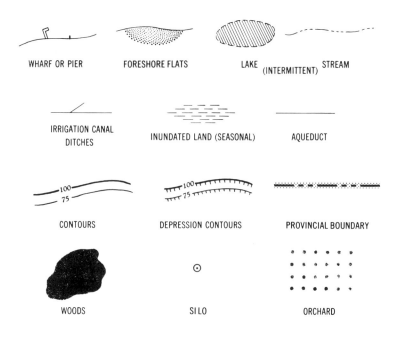

| WHARF OR PIER | FORESHORE FLATS | LAKE (INTERMITTENT) | STREAM |

| IRRIGATION CANAL DITCHES | INUNDATED LAND (SEASONAL) | AQUEDUCT |

| CONTOURS | DEPRESSION CONTOURS | PROVINCIAL BOUNDARY |

| WOODS | SILO | ORCHARD |

Figure 2-3   Road Symbols as Found on Topographical Maps

hard surface, all weather

dual highway   more than 2 lanes

hard surface, all weather

2 lanes   less than 2 lanes

loose or stabilized surface, all weather

2 lanes or more   less than 2 lanes

loose surface, dry weather and
unclassified streets

cart track

trail or portage

37

Line symbols show features that have length but little width, such as roads, trails, fences, rivers, streams, and power lines. Also included in this category are line symbols representing features that cannot be seen on the ground but are, nevertheless, very important. These include contours (lines of equal elevation) that indicate hills, valleys, and administrative boundaries.

Area symbols, as the name implies, are those that cover an appreciable area on the map. These symbols each have two components: an outline indicating the extent of the feature and a distinctive tint or pattern indicating the nature of the feature. For example, a marsh on coloured maps has a broken blue outline to show that it is wet (blue for water) and that the marsh edge may change with the season. (Hence the breaks in the indefinite outline.) Other area symbols are for lakes, ponds, forests, tundra, dunes, sandpits, quarries, and wide rivers.

Figure 2-4   Illustration of a Hill and Its Contours

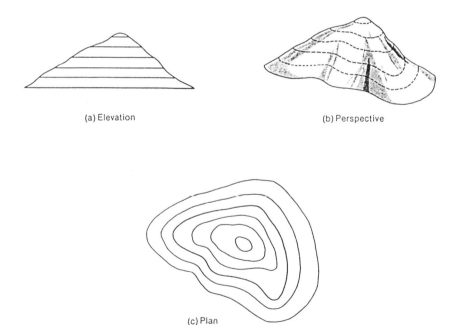

(a) Elevation

(b) Perspective

(c) Plan

Figure 2-5 Illustration of an Imaginary Hill Which Rises from Sea Level to 158 Feet.

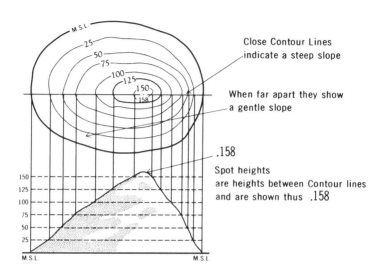

On most Canadian coloured topographical maps, the colours used are:

Blue: water features including lakes, rivers, marshes, pools, springs, glaciers

Green: vegetation such as woods, orchards, hedges, landmark trees, vineyards

Brown: all depiction of relief by contours and symbols for cliffs, sandpits, dunes

Black: the majority of man-made features such as buildings, railroads, quarries

Red: paved roads, the built-up areas of towns and cities

Orange: gravel roads.

Some symbols are printed in tints of the above basic colours.

One of the most important attributes of a topographical map is that it portrays the shape of the ground. It shows the location of hills and flatlands and more importantly, it allows the map user to determine the actual height of the hills, the steepness of roads, and even the view from a hilltop. The shape of the ground has an important effect on the shape and location of the other topographical features. It determines the course of rivers and streams, the density and shape of road patterns and even, to some extent, the location of towns and villages.

The *datum plane* is the reference point from which all the heights on the map are measured. On Canadian maps, it almost always means sea level, which is the average level of the sea through all changes of the tide. The elevation of a point on a topographical map is its vertical distance above mean sea level.

The most common way of indicating relief is by *contour lines*. A contour line is the representation on a map of an imaginary line on the ground along which all points have the same elevation. If a person walked along a contour line he would go neither up nor down, but would stay at a constant elevation. Another way to visualize contours is to imagine a hill cut into horizontal slices. The plan drawing of the edge of each slice is a contour (see Figure 2-4, Illustration of a Hill and Its Contours).

You will find topographical maps very useful in locating the property, in visualizing contours, and in estimating the steepness of hills. These maps also make excellent road maps because of the wealth of details they contain, details that never appear on ordinary maps. You will identify sideroads, railroad tracks, school houses, bridges, cemeteries, creeks, small lakes – all in their precise location. Fishermen and hunters can use the maps to speculate on likely locations for game, and the best means of access to remote areas. Campers can visualize suitable sites, removed from well-beaten paths.

Proficiency in map reading comes only with practice in the field. When one has acquired this proficiency, it is quite possible to obtain from a map a clear picture of a specific area without actually seeing it.

If your province uses the lots and concession system to describe tax arrear properties, you will find that matching a topographical map with a county map can help you get a clearer picture of the properties listed in tax sale notices.

While your topographic maps will not show township lots, they will come close to showing you the concessions, particularly on maps depicting areas on a larger scale. You may have difficulty seeing the concessions at first but you should be able to find the township you are interested in without any difficulty. Once you have found the township, look carefully for a row of Roman numerals running one under the other at regular intervals between the township boundaries. Set your county map beside your topographical map. With a ruler, you will be able to pencil in the concession with reasonable accuracy by putting the pencil lines midway between the Roman numerals.

You could do the same with the lot lines for the areas that interest you, using landmarks and roads as general guidelines. Now open your eyes and begin to see what is there. Your topographical map contains symbols for various features such as schools, bridges, swamps, types of roads, cliffs, hills, rivers, streams, etc.... Is the area wooded? Swampy? Hilly? Built up? Isolated? Is there road access? What landmarks can help you find the exact spot?

You can obtain topographical maps from the Federal Government, official publisher of all topographical maps. Write to:

> The Canada Map Office
> Department of Energy Mines and Resources
> 615 Booth Street
> Ottawa, Ont., K1A OE9

The Canada Map Office requires prepayment for all maps. Payment should be made by cheque or money order, payable to the Receiver General for Canada. Prices for maps do change often and therefore, we recommend that you inquire about prices before ordering.

12

Air Photography

An aerial photograph is any photo taken from the air. All of Canada has been photographed from the air – some parts of it many times over, in different seasons, at different scales, and in different years going back to the 1920's.

Air photos often give information concerning the nature of the land and data which is not available from map study alone.

An aerial photograph can have several advantages over a line map.

- It provides a pictorial representation of the ground that is infinitely more detailed than on a line map. This is of great importance in wilderness areas where there are few, if any, man-made features and where natural land patterns can be identified on both the photograph and the ground.

- Aerial photos are often more up to date than the most recent map of the area.

- Aerial photographs provide a detailed record of changes in the topography. Such a record is valuable for historical and geographical research.

Consequently, air photography is another valuable source of information for the properties you have in mind. Aerial photos are not recommended in most cases, yet, in a few instances, you may want to have the additional information. The property might be large and densely forested, or it might lie under several feet of snow. A picture taken from the air can present you with a completely different perspective.

A remarkable amount of information can be obtained from aerial photos. If you order pairs of photos, i.e. "stereo pairs", and take them to an expert such as a forestry engineer, an agricultural expert, or a land surveyor, he will have the stereoscopic viewer

Figure 2-6 Illustration of Pocket Stereoscope

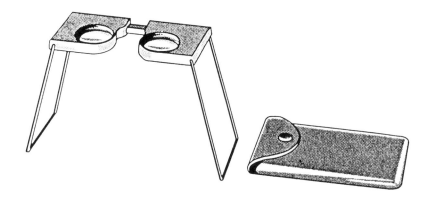

Figure 2-7 Placement of Stereoscope in Order to View Two Overlapping Photos.

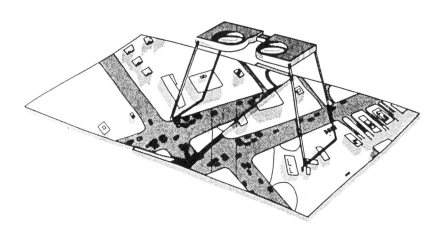

necessary to read your photos. He can tell you the type and size of timber growing on the land and the depth and type of soil; he can identify potential spots for gravel pits, existing roads, hills, valleys, ridges, etc.... He can also see the slope of the ground and determine whether the land is dry or wet. The features all show up in a three dimensional format.

Learning to "read" air photos takes time and practice. To master the technique, purchase a stereoscopic pair of photographs of some interesting area near your home. Buy or borrow a pocket stereoscope (illustrated in Figure 2-6). Obtain a topographical map covering the area shown on your photos and, as a first exercise, examine the features that have been identified on the map. Look for differences in appearance between paved, gravel, and dirt roads. If there is a marsh in the area, see how it differs from dry ground. Note the varying appearances of the cultivated fields and think of what might cause this difference. Finally, when you have exhausted the study of your sample area, go onto the ground and confirm your interpretation.

Air photos can also be obtained in non-stereo coverage. For many, this is more than sufficient, as they also provide a complete picture of the area.

The aerial photo and the topographical map, when used together, form a powerful investigative instrument in the study of any region's physical geography.

How To Order Aerial Photographs:

1. Obtain a topographical map of the area you wish to study from a local map dealer (check yellow pages of telephone directory) or from the Canada Map Office, 615 Booth St., Ottawa, Ont., K1A OE9

2. Mark very precisely on the topographical map the land area you want photographed.

3. Indicate what specific features you want visible on the photo (i.e. lake, hill, road, house, etc...) and whether your main criteria is detail or scale.

4. Include the following data.

   • Name, address, and telephone number.

   • Do you require stereoscopic coverage?

- The reason for the photograph. (The Air Photo Library may make suggestions and recommendations as to what best suits your requirements.)
- Type of print needed:
  - Full negative (23 by 23 cm) or an enlargement
  - Colour or black and white
  - Latest photography or photograph taken closest to a particular date
  - Small scale (greater area) or large scale (more detail)
  - On transparency or paper.

One can obtain aerial photos for any area in Canada from the

> National Air Photo Library
> 615 Booth Street
> Ottawa, Ontario
> KlA OE9

One can also obtain aerial photos and other maps from each province. (See Appendix C for addresses of provincial map offices.)

Cost for maps vary. We suggest that you write or telephone to determine current pricing.

## 13

How To Tell If You Have Enough Information

L et us assume that you now have the required maps and have followed the procedures outlined to date. For some listings, you may have enough information. However, if the description reads

Pt. Lot 12, Conc. 9

or

Lot 11, Block 3, Plan 21125

or

Lot 35, Block 2, District Lot 202,
Plan 55LD37, Group One NWD

you will have to do a bit more research to understand what is being described. Unless the municipality provides you with a street address and/or gives you a package which contains specific information about the property, such as lot dimensions, street address and/or a sketch of the parcel in question, further research will be mandatory. As you can see from the above legal descriptions, it can be difficult to get a clear picture of the property.

Take a day off, gather all your maps, lists, photocopies, and other information, and drive to the town or city where the Land Titles or Registry Office is located. Addresses for most of these offices can be found in the Canadian Almanac and Directory(see Section 18).There are many Land Titles and Registry Offices scattered throughout the country. A phone call to your local municipality will help you determine the address of the office(s) in the area you wish to explore.

You should plan on spending half a day, maybe longer at this office. The length of your stay will depend on the number of properties you want to explore. Most Land Titles and Registry Offices are open from 9:00 a.m. to 4:30 p.m.. It is a good idea to go at least a week or two before the sale because, as the date of the sale approaches, the office can become crowded with other interested researchers, and you could find a slowdown in the service.

14

Land Titles and Registry Offices

P rior to the advent of public registration, ownership of land was identified and proven by a collection of title documents kept by each owner of land in his personal deed box. The purchaser acquired the historical record when he bought the land and added his deed to the collection of previous deeds passed on. Therefore, in order to prove ownership, it was necessary to show that you were the present owner of the last deed which had its "chain" commencing with the grant from the Crown. This method, of course, was fraught with difficulties and it quickly became clear that some form of central registry should be devised.

Accordingly, each province established Land Titles and Registry Offices. These offices continue to exist and the record of ownership of all land, from the date upon which the original grant from the Crown was given to the present, is available for inspection by the public. The various records kept and the methods of registration have changed drastically over the years, but the essentials remain and the concept of registering documents has not changed.

Land Titles and Registry Offices keep a series of books in which each transaction is entered and have on file, for future examination, the original or microfilm of each document tendered for registration. Each document is micro-filmed should the original become misplaced or destroyed.

For much of Canada, in particular western Canada, real estate documents and transactions are recorded in Land Titles Offices. On the other hand, many eastern provinces use a method called the Registry System. Some provinces, such as Ontario, use both the Land Titles System and the Registry System. Gradually, more and more provinces are moving towards the Land Titles System for registering all real estate transactions. The latter is considered to be the most efficient of the two methods.

It is important to note that methods and procedures for the recording of real estate transactions vary not only between provinces but also between different offices within each province.

If, after consulting with the municipality holding the tax sale, you have not been able to obtain all the information you need, you can usually obtain the following information at the Land Titles or Registry Office:

- lot size and dimensions
- whether there are easements or rights of way attached to the property
- the last selling price of the property.

A Word of Caution

Using Land Titles and Registry Offices is not for everyone. Quite often, obtaining the required documents can prove to be an easy task. However, the experience can also be quite frustrating because some legal descriptions make it difficult to pinpoint the parcel in question, especially under the Registry System. Title searching is a specialized field and there are people who make this a full-time occupation. In most communities, you will be able to find someone who will do this type of work for you and charge an hourly fee. (Most searches cost between $45.00 and $60.00.) The Land Titles and/or Registry Offices should be able to refer you to someone who works as a title searcher. As well, by consulting the yellow pages of your telephone directory under "Searchers of Records" or "Title Searchers", you will find individuals or businesses who specialize in this type of work. The money spent for this type of assistance might be well worth it.

Using the Land Titles and/or Registry Office is perhaps the most challenging aspect of the property search. Initially, you may find it somewhat time consuming and even confusing, but once you understand the basics, the skills acquired will serve you well in subsequent searches.

15
Using Registry Offices

hat you are ultimately trying to find in the Registry Office is the deed to the registered owner to see how the property is described.

If the deed, instrument, or R-Plan numbers are included in the tax sale notice, move on to the heading entitled "Getting the Required Document".

If, in the tax sale listings, no deed, instrument, or R-Plan numbers were given, you will need to go through the steps outlined in the following paragraphs.

Finding the Deed, Instrument, or R-Plan

Select one of the properties you have decided to explore further and present the legal description of the property to the Registry Office desk. In all likelihood, you will be presented with a large *Abstract Book*. (In order to obtain any document or book you will have to fill in a request form and pay a small fee.) You will notice that each page of the Abstract Book is partitioned into headings such as Date, Grantor, Grantee, Description, etc. . . . (See Sample 2-2, Page From an Abstract Book.)

Thumb through the book until you reach the property in question. Examine the most recent entries. When you have found the last entries, look in the column headed *Instrument*. Go up this column searching for the word *Grant, Deed*, or *Transfer*. When you find one of these headings, go across this row until you locate the name of the *Grantee* (the owner). Keep going across this row until you get to the legal description of the property.

If, in the *Description* column there is reference to an *R-Plan* make note of this R-Plan number. (You will want to refer to it shortly.) R-plans for properties split into lots after 1973 should be on file.

Getting the Required Documents

On the appropriate Registry Office form, enter the R-Plan number and/or deed registration number and give them to the person at the desk. He/She will bring you these documents. Cross-check these documents against the name or reference number (Ex: Instrument, R-Plan, etc. . .) on the tax sale list and the notes you have made. If an R-Plan is provided, you may find that it is all you need in order to determine the dimensions and characteristics of the parcel in question.

For deeds and/or instruments, verify that you have indeed been given the right number. Remember, what you seek to obtain from these documents is a description of the property.

Sample 2-2   Page From an Abstract Book

LOT 31   CONCESSION 12

REGISTRATION NUMBER	INSTRUMENT	DATE OF INSTRUMENT	REGISTRATION DATE (DAY MONTH YEAR)	GRANTOR	GRANTEE	CONSIDERATION ETC.	LAND AND REMARKS
N364815	MORT		25 01 88	Cochrane, Samuel John	Bank of Montreal	$100,000.00	Pt. being Pt. 1 on 5R-7569
	Discharged by #N431756 Asst. Dep. Land Reg. Lg. 29-05-88.						
N366860	CONST LIEN		10 02 88	Cochrane, Anna Claire	Jeff Moore Excavating Ltd.	$4,288.00	Pt. being Pt. 2 on 5R-7569
N368782	MORT		01 03 88	Cochrane, Anna Claire	Bank of Montreal	$81,500.00	Pt. being Pt. 2 on 5R-7569
	Discharged by #N439977 Asst. Dep. Land Reg. Lg. 01/06/88.						
N368783	MORT		01 03 88	Cochrane, Anna Claire	Bank of Montreal	$100,000.00	Pt. being Pt. 2 on 5R-7569
	Discharged by #N447587 Asst. Dep. Land Reg. Lg. 18/07/88.						
N368991	POWER OF ATTORNEY		01 03 88	Sherman Rosa Marie	Sharma, Anil		Pt. being Pt. 1 on 5R-7569
N368992	GRANT		01 03 88	Cochrane, Samuel John	Sharma, Rosaleen Frances	$227,000.00	Pt. being Pt. 1 on 5R-7569. As in inst. NS337953.
N368993	MORT		01 03 88	Sherman Rosa Marie	National Trust Co.	$170,000.00	See no. N444002.
	Discharged by #N465744 Asst. Dep. Land Reg. Lg. 21/11/88.						
N369214	ORDER		02 03 88	SCO			Vacating Const Lien N366860
N371486	CERT OF ACTION	25 03 88	SCO	Jeff Moore Excavating Ltd.			Re: Const Lien N366860.
N380752	MORT		03 06 88	Cochrane, Anna	Bank of Montreal	$170,000.00	Pt of W 1/2, being pt 2 on 5R-7569. As in NS337951.
N380899	MORT		03 06 88	Sherman Rosa Marie	CIBC Mort. Corp.	$138,889.28	Pt being Pt 1 on 5R-7569

Sometimes the property description can be quite straightforward, but at other times it can be confusing because of the particular jargon used to describe certain parcels of land. Occasionally, you may find a detailed surveyor's description which could be several pages long (See Sample 2-3, Surveyor's Description). If this should be the case, check to see if the surveyor has included a sketch of the worded description. If there is a sketch, breathe a sigh of relief as it will save you much time and energy. Copy the sketch and file it with your notes for that piece of property.

If, on the other hand, no sketch exists, you will have to try to decipher the surveyor's description and draw a sketch from this worded description. If it is your first attempt at deciphering such a description, you should seek the help of someone who does this type of work. Many people in the building are working as title searchers and are quite skilled at seeing through these surveyor's descriptions. Frequently, there are people present who work on contract or by the hour and would be willing to offer their services for an hour or so. The money spent for this type of assistance would be worth it in terms of the experience gained. After you have received help a few times, you will be able to handle most descriptions on your own.

When your sketches are complete and you have copied the relevant information, turn to the end of the deed and look for a statement which reveals the price paid (sometimes called the "Consideration") for this parcel of land. Note the date of the transaction. Keep this information with your notes as it should help you determine how much you will bid for this property.

## 16

Using Land Titles Offices

L and Titles Offices rely on large books called *parcel registers* in order to record information. Each book contains a particular concession (sometimes called a "range" or "section") or registered plan for the municipality, with separate pages for each lot in the concession or on the plan. For each division of property created, a new page is added to the parcel register.

The Land Titles parcel register has a record of every instrument (document) that was ever registered against the property. However, all documents that are superceded by newer restrictions are crossed off and only the entries not crossed off are deemed to apply to the title. For example, if person X sells to person Y in 1990 and then person Y sells to person Z in 1992, when person Y's transfer is recorded in the Land Titles book, the 1990 transfer to person Y will be crossed off. If person Y had a mortgage that was paid off at the time of the sale to person Z, that mortgage would also be crossed off in the book. If person Z then went and secured his own mortgage, it would be entered into the parcel register.

If there are easements, liens or other restrictions affecting the lot, they will appear in the parcel register and get crossed off once they no longer apply to the property.

With the Land Titles System, the Land Registrar certifies that the land is affected only by those documents (liens, easements, mortgages, etc. . .) that are not crossed off. The Land Registrar can do this because the property underwent an exhaustive examination of title before it was registered with the Land Titles System. Anyone registering property for the first time with the Land Titles System must demonstrate that there are no old mortgages, deeds, etc. . . which might affect the title to the property.

Any new parcels or lots created must be surveyed and a reference plan must be submitted for approval.

The Land Registrar charges a hefty fee for first time registrations. A portion of this fee is used to establish an insurance fund for the protection of authorities should legal action be taken because of some error or omission in the registration of title.

With the Land Titles System, you will generally not be given an original copy of the documents requested. Instead, you will be provided with a microfilm version which can in turn be photocopied using most microfilm viewing machines.

On the standard request form, fill in the legal description (see Section 13 for examples of legal descriptions) as given in the tax sale notice. This should be sufficient for you to receive the *parcel register*. In the *parcel register* you will find a reference number for an R-Plan (see Sample 2-4, R-Plan), if one exists. If none is available, there should be a reference to a surveyor's description (see Sample 2-3, Surveyor's Description). Obtain copies of these documents in order to determine the dimensions and other characteristics of the property(ies) in question.

Look for the word "transfer" in the parcel register. Here you will often find an entry which indicates the price previously paid for the parcel.

Look for the words "agreement" or "notices of agreement" and you will find reference to a document which will help you determine if there are restrictions, easements, or rights of way attached to the property. It may be necessary to consult the original document in order to fully understand the implications of the aforementioned.

Having discovered this information, you are now in a better position to determine whether the property(ies) you have been searching is worth further consideration.

Sample 2-3 Surveyor's Description

In the Province of Ontario, in the County of Frontenac, in the Township of Wolfe Island, and being composed of part of Lot 8, Concession 8, South of the Base Line, and which said parcel or tract of land may be more particularly described as follows:

PREMISING THAT the bearings herein are astronomic, derived from King's Highway No. 95 as shown on Deposited Plan No. 806 and are referred to the meridian through the intersection of the Base Line with the centre line of the road allowance between Concessions 9 and 10, Township of Wolfe Island, and relating all bearings herein thereto.

COMMENCING at a survey bar planted on the east limit of Lot 8 a distance of 233.28 feet and bearing north 32 degrees, 10 minutes, 30 seconds west from the southeast corner of Lot 8, Concession 8 South of the Base Line.

THENCE south 58 degrees, 49 minutes, 30 seconds west a distance of 300.00 feet to a survey bar planted, said survey bar marking the point of commencement of the herein described parcel of land.

THENCE CONTINUING south 58 degrees, 49 minutes, 30 seconds west a distance of 100.00 feet to a survey bar planted.

THENCE south 32 degrees, 10 minutes, 30 seconds east a distance of 251.95 feet to a survey bar planted.

THENCE CONTINUING south 32 degrees, 10 minutes, 30 seconds east a distance of 19 feet plus or minus to the high water mark of the St. Lawrence River.

THENCE easterly along the high water mark of the St. Lawrence River a distance of 100 feet plus or minus to the point of intersection of a line drawn south 32 degrees, 10 minutes, 30 seconds east from the point of commencement.

THENCE north 32 degrees, 10 minutes, 30 seconds west a distance of 20 feet plus or minus to a survey bar planted.

THENCE CONTINUING north 32 degrees, 10 minutes, 30 seconds west a distance of 250.00 feet to the point of commencement, subject to a right-of-way to all those entitled over the south 20 feet of the north 80 feet of the above-described parcel of land, and which said parcel is shown outlined in heavy lines on a plan of survey by Ray Hunter, O.L.S., dated April 22,1972.

TOGETHER WITH a right-a-way with all those entitled thereto over a strip of land 20 feet wide and which said right-of-way may be located as follows:

COMMENCING at a survey bar planted on the east limit of Lot 8 a distance of 153.28 feet and bearing north 32 degrees, 10 minutes, 30 seconds west from the southeast corner of Lot 8, Concession 8, South of the Base Line.

THENCE south 58 degrees, 49 minutes, 30 seconds west a distance of 300.00 feet to a survey bar planted.

THENCE north 32 degrees, 10 minutes, 30 seconds west a distance of 20.00 feet to a survey bar planted.

THENCE north 58 degrees, 49 minutes, 30 seconds east a distance of 300.00 feet to a survey bar planted on the east limit of Lot 8.

THENCE south 32 degrees, 10 minutes, 30 seconds east a distance of 20.00 feet to the point of commencement, and which said parcel is shown outlined in heavy lines on a plan of survey by Ray Hunter, Ontario Land Surveyor, dated April, 1972.

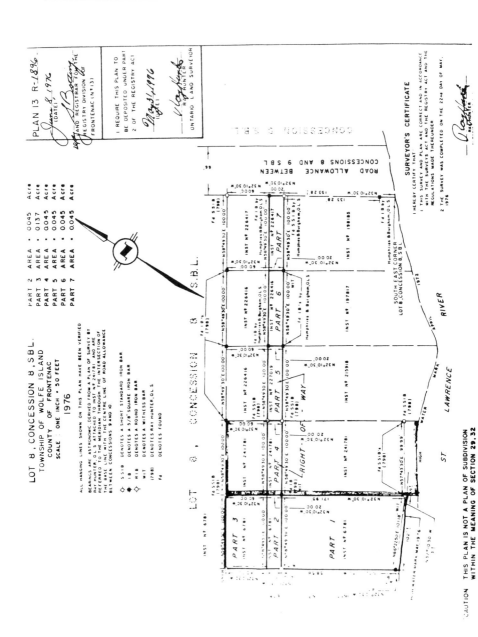

56

## 17

Using the Assessment Department

A ssessment is the valuation of property for tax purposes only. It is not the selling price of property. In assessing, the assessor is trying to arrive at an equitable method of valuing property so that all similar properties are given the same value. The assessed value is used in computing the amount of property tax payable. The rate of tax, or mill rate (a mill is 1/10 of one cent) is applied to the assessment to arrive at the amount of tax. If, for example, your property is assessed at $10,000 and the mill rate is 50, the annual tax would be $500.

Surprisingly, you can discover a great deal of information about a particular piece of property and its owner simply by consulting the local municipal assessment rolls. If you want to learn some details about Mr. and Mrs. Spratt's property, just drop in at the area assessment office. Give Mr. Spratt's address to the clerk on duty and he/she will provide you with a large assessment volume which will answer many of your questions.

The volume will not give any particulars on the purchase price, mortgages, liens, etc. . . . You should have obtained this information when you explored the deed at the Land Titles or Registry Office. It will, however, give the assessed value of the property and many other interesting details such as the following:

- Municipality
- Ward Number
- Assessment roll number
- Official property address with lot and concession number

- Class of property – residential, vacation, commercial

- Lot frontage

- Lot depth

- Whether the property is developed or vacant land

- Whether the occupant is owner or tenant

- School support status.

Addresses and telephone numbers for all Ontario assessment offices can be found in the CANADIAN ALMANAC and DIRECTORY.

18
Canadian Almanac and Directory

T hroughout this book, we have frequently referred to the Canadian Almanac and Directory as being a useful tool in helping you learn more about the various properties selling for non-payment of taxes. The Canadian Almanac and Directory is published annually and can be consulted free of charge at most public libraries. It is available through some bookstores and can also be purchased from

Canadian Almanac and Directory
2775 Matheson Blvd. E.
Mississauga, Ontario
L4W 4P7

You will be surprised at the cost of this directory – over $100.00 – and may prefer to consult it at your local library. Though expensive, it is a thorough publication which contains a wealth of information about your country. It contains

- the address, telephone number, population figures, name of either the clerk or treasurer (person to contact when making enquiries about a tax sale in a specific municipality) of every municipality throughout Canada (see Sample 2-5)

- the address and telephone number for every Canadian newspaper and magazine

- a listing of every federal and provincial government department – listed alphabetically under topics of frequent need and interest. (In this section, you will find addresses and phone numbers of the major Land Titles and Registry Offices. You will also find addresses to obtain maps in each province

- maps showing the different North American time zones, solar and lunar tables, planetary configurations, list of abbreviations, etc. . . . .

This is but a sampling of the information contained in this 1250 page publication.

Sample 2-5 Page from The Canadian Almanac and Directory

BRITISH COLUMBIA MUNICIPALITIES

Cities in CAPITALS; District municipality marked †; Towns marked ‡; Balance are villages.
Area Code for British Columbia is 604

MUNICIPALITY	1988 POP	COUNTY OR DISTRICT	FEDERAL ELECTORAL DISTRICT	PROVINCIAL ELECTORAL DISTRICT	CLERK WITH ADDRESS & PHONE
Midway	640	Kootenay Boundary	Okanagan-Similkameen-Merritt	Boundary-Similkameen	Robert J. Hatton, Village Clerk, PO Box 160, Midway, BC V0H 1M0 (449-2222)
Mission †	21,985	Dewdney-Alouette	Mission-Coquitlam	Dewdney	Donald West, Dist. Mun. Clerk, PO Box 20, Mission, BC V2V 4L9 (826-6271)
Montrose	1,183	Kootenay Boundary	Kootenay-West Revelstoke	Rossland-Trail	Gerry A. Henke, Village Clerk, PO Box 510, Montrose, BC V0G 1P0 (367-7234)
Nakusp	1,410	Central Kootenay	Kootenay-West-Revelstoke	Nelson-Creston	C. Froese, Village Clerk, PO Box 280, Nakusp, BC V0G 1R0 (265-3689)
NANAIMO	49,029	Nanaimo	Nanaimo-Cowichan	Nanaimo	Gary C. Nason, City Clerk, 455 Wallace St., Nanaimo, BC V9R 5J6 (754-4251)
NELSON	8,113	Central Kootenay	Kootenay West-Revelstoke	Nelson-Creston	Douglas Ormond, City Clerk, 502 Vernon St., Nelson, BC V1L 4E8 (352-5511)
New Denver	596	Central Kootenay	Kootenay West-Revelstoke	Nelson-Creston	Vera Hamilton, Village Clerk, PO Box 40, New Denver, BC V0G 1S0 (358-2316)
New Hazelton †	796	Kitmat-Stikine	Skeena	Skeena	Betty Hunt, Dist. Mun. Clerk, PO Box 340, New Hazelton, BC V0J 2J0 (842-6571)
NEW WESTMINSTER	39,972	Greater Vancouver	New Westminster-Burnaby	New Westminster	Cathy Bruce, City Clerk, 511 Royal Ave., New Westminster, BC V3L 1H9 (521-3711)
North Cowichan †	18,674	Cowichan Valley	Nanaimo-Cowichan	Cowichan-Malahat	James Dias, Dist. Mun. Clerk, PO Box 278, Duncan, BC V9L 3X4 (746-7101)
North Saanich †	7,247	Capital	Saanich-Gulf Islands	Saanich & the Islands	Joan Schill, Dist. Mun. Clerk, PO Box 2639, Sidney, BC V8L 4C1 (656-0781)

Seeing the Property And Getting Ready For the Sale

Now To See the Actual Piece of Property

Y ou have finally completed your research. You now have a good idea of the type, size, location, and value of the property(ies). You are ready to see the actual piece of property. Allow a full day or more for this part of your research. Driving to and locating each property will take time, perhaps more than you anticipated.

Keep a file on each property so that you remain organized.

If you are visiting unfamiliar territories, you will need to study your topographical map carefully as it will be your best guide. You will be amazed by its accuracy and usefulness and its incredible amount of detail. When you approach the area you want to explore, drive slowly, studying the landmarks carefully and looking closely at your sketches for key points. Use the symbols on your topographical map to find large buildings, schools, churches, railways, hills, cliffs, forest, trails, etc. . . . Check the map for the number of kilometers you must cover and then keep an eye on your car's mileage gauge. If you have driven twenty kilometers and you should have spotted the property after ten kilometers, you know you have gone too far.

Estimating the Value
of a Property

T he time will come when you have thoroughly re-searched a property and decide to submit a tender (or bid at the auction), but before doing so, you should carefully estimate the value of the property.

Determining the value of a piece of land (developed or vacant) can be a difficult and complicated process. Included in this section is a list of factors which affect the value of a property and sources to contact for specific data on the property and surrounding area.

Often, value is determined by the simple law of supply and demand: the greater the interest in a particular type of property and the less of it there is, the greater the value will be. However, value does not depend only on supply and demand but on many other elements such as:

– usability (e.g. flat land is more valuable)

– clearness of title (e.g. is it encumbered by liens, right of ways, etc. . .)

– picture quality (e.g. the view, the architecture, the land-scaping)

– frontage along a road or waterway

– zoning and building codes

– climate

– age and condition of the buildings

– location (e.g. schools, shopping areas, church, public transportation, neighbours, etc...)

- size of the property in question
- exposure (e.g. when does it get sun, where are the prevailing winds)
- utilities and their availability
- vegetation and quality of the soil
- maintenance of the property
- drainage
- quality and quantity of water
- accessibility (e.g. quality of the roads, can these be kept open year round?)
- growth in the area (e.g. economic, industrial, population).

Each of the above can contribute to increasing or decreasing the value of a property. Frequently, a piece of real estate located close to a populated area is considered more desirable and therefore, it will be more expensive. If it has a picture postcard view, fronts along water, is close to all conveniences, and is easily accessible by road, it will have more value than property which does not have these characteristics.

Another key factor to consider in setting value is the potential for development. The property has value not so much for what it is now but for what it can become in the future. If the growth in a particular city is occurring in the direction of the parcel in question, there is greater potential for it to increase in value, especially if it is flat land that lends itself well to subdivision development. If you are looking at rural property, keep in mind that if the land has stands of timber, it has more potential than land that is somewhat rocky and sparse in vegetation. It doesn't really matter whether you plan to use that timber or not. The potential is there should you wish to cut down the trees. In setting value, always be sure to consider the potential use of the parcel and try to determine how soon the property will come in demand for this use. The municipal tax office (assessment department) may be able to provide some information on this matter, for these officials often know about planned land developments in the area and their possible effect on land value.

Where can you obtain more specific information on the property? Well, one possible source of information is the municipal tax office (assessment department). From this office, you can obtain an assessor's evaluation of the market value of the property. The municipality has used this specific information to determine the amount of taxes payable. Looking at the assessed value and multiplying it by the mill rate will tell you the taxes due each year. By doing these calculations for other properties in the same area, you can get an idea of the value assigned to this property in relation to others of similar size and characteristics.

Another possible source of information is your local real estate agency. Real estate agents are usually familiar with land prices for most areas. They will know the selling price for properties sold in that area in the recent past and will probably be able to explain why parcels of similar size sold for different prices.

Each piece of real estate is unique and value may have increased depending on improvements made. Or, where two properties are similar in size and location, the price will vary greatly, perhaps because one property has a beautiful spring fed stream running through it.

Once you have discovered the selling price of a few properties in your area of interest, you can use something called the "comparison test" to determine the market value of the property you wish to bid on. If other local properties, being similar in size and features, are worth a certain amount, then this property is also worth about the same number of dollars.

If the property sold within the last few years and you cannot obtain any information on the selling price from a real estate agent, try the Land Titles or Registry Office. Do not forget to bring the legal description with you. (This is the description of the property as it appeared in the local newspaper or provincial gazette.) A clerk will help you find the appropriate document, which is the last registered deed or transfer. Consequently, you will have some idea of the value of the property at the time of the last sale.

One final means of estimating the value of the property is to hire an appraiser. You should note that the sources of information consulted by appraisers are also available to the public. If the appraiser has worked for a number of years in your area of interest, he will be thoroughly familiar with property values. If you should decide to go this route you can expect his report to include:

- an evaluation of the house and other buildings
- perhaps comparison figures on other similar sales in the area
- comments on
  • value of the location
  • anticipated economic and population growth
  • known restrictions
- present and future zoning possibilities
- availability of utilities and other services.

(if he/she has access to the building)

- comments on
  • electrical system
  • plumbing
  • heating system
  • size of rooms
  • etc. . . . .

## 21

Do I Get Clear Title?

T he question often arises as to whether or not a successful bidder gets clear title to properties purchased at tax sales. At times, tax sale notices conclude with a paragraph similar to the following.

"The municipality makes no representation regarding the title to or any other matters relating to the land to be sold. Responsibility for ascertaining these matters rests with the potential purchasers".

Clear title is indeed granted, subject to certain qualifications. The successful purchaser receives a deed to the property and this is considered to be the granting of clear title. But, this clear title does not remove any easements or covenants (such as Hydro right of way or right of crossing held by the owner of the neighbouring property) attached to the property. It does, however, remove any liens or mortgages. Anyone having a financial interest in the property (such as a mortgage holder) is advised well ahead of any tax sale and has plenty of time to take action if he/she so wishes.

Should you want to determine if easements or covenants are attached to the property, you will need to do a search at the Registry or Land Titles Office. We have outlined steps in Chapter Two of this book to guide any individual wanting to do his own search.

If you do not feel confident enough to do the title search yourself, you can seek the help of companies that specialize in title searching. Simply consult the yellow pages of your telephone directory for "Searchers of Records". They usually charge an hourly fee for their services. This is money well spent since it will give you peace of mind when the time comes to submit your tender or bid at an auction.

Title searching is not for everyone and it is a procedure you may wish to avoid completely. Many will prefer to consult with a lawyer in all matters related to purchasing property. Though not necessary, legal counsel can be reassuring for any potential purchaser.

Will I Be Able To Obtain a Building Permit?

In the case of vacant land, it is the purchaser's responsibility to determine whether it is possible to build on the parcel in question. The municipality holding the sale will generally have the answer to that question. If they do not, it will be necessary to check with the appropriate municipal zoning department.

22

Public Auctions

A s was previously mentioned, tax sales are held by public auction and sometimes by public tender. Our present focus will be on auctions. The auction procedure is used not only to dispose of tax arrear properties, but to sell other types of properties and general merchandise. In fact auctions are advertised almost weekly under the Public Notices section of your newspaper. Since preparation is almost always the key to success, we are offering the following guidelines for anyone who has intentions of attending auctions.

- Be aware that it is the auctioneer's responsibility to obtain the highest bid possible. With some types of auctions the auctioneer will receive a commission on what he sells.

- It is best to attend several auctions before making any serious bids. You need to get a "feel" for the process so use your first auctions as a way of observing and assessing how others behave. When you attend your first tax sale auction, or any auction, you will notice that as the time of sale approaches, the auction room becomes quite crowded. You will also observe that most of the people attending the auction are there as spectators only; a very small percentage will actually make a bid. You will soon become familiar with the tempo; the auctioneer is quick and efficient. Bids will sometimes last one minute and have only one interested bidder, or, at other times, bidding can go on for ten minutes while bidders outdo one another with small sums of five to ten dollars.

– Always research the property (or inspect the merchandise) for which you are contemplating placing a bid. If you don't feel that you know enough about the property in question, then resist making a bid. (Better safe than sorry.)

– Be sure to read and understand the conditions of sale before making a bid. It may require some time and effort but you will eliminate the chances of disappointment afterwards.

– Always bring cash, certified cheques, or money orders to any auction at which you are planning to make a purchase. At all tax sales, the successful bidder is expected to pay his bid immediately after the sale closes. Payment is generally required in either cash or certified cheque. We strongly recommend that you do not carry a large bundle of cash. A certified cheque is excellent, or you might consider traveller's cheques.

– Never go beyond a predetermined limit when bidding. Base this limit on the information you have gathered. Avoid becoming obsessed with an item. Doing so will lead you to bid more than the property (or merchandise) is worth. If you are bidding on a tax arrear property, you might bring a certified cheque for the maximum amount you intent to bid. This should ensure that you do not get carried away with the bidding process. If you are the successful bidder and the property is sold for less than the amount on your cheque, the clerk/treasurer will issue a refund for the difference.

- Avoid catching *auction fever*. This happens when bidders get carried away with the process; they will bid on anything and everything that is being auctioned and often will end up being the owner of things they did not even want and paying far too much for these items. The opposite of auction fever is *auction paralysis*. This occurs when the bidder is paralysed with fear and thus is unable to make a bid. Apparently such a state is often due to a fear of overpaying. If you don't overcome it you will never get started. Often, if you fail to do your homework, you will not have the confidence to bid.

- When the time comes for you to make your first bid, make it ridiculously low. Don't worry about what others will think. The crowd might become puzzled but no one will single you out for embarrassment. Then sit back and see how much the item actually sells for. Did it go for a great deal more than your initial low bid? How many bidders were involved from beginning to end? How did the last few bidders conduct themselves? Did they follow a strategy? This approach will break the ice and give you the confidence necessary to make future bids.

PLEASE NOTE: When you have questions regarding a particular sale you should direct these to the local official (Clerk or Treasurer) mentioned on the tax sale lists. He is the one who is responsible for hosting the sale. Answers to certain questions may vary with different locations and what may be true for one municipality or township may vary slightly in another.

## Chapter Four

Buying
Country
Property

Many properties sold at tax sales are located outside major cities. For this reason, we have included a chapter detailing the many factors which should be considered when purchasing rural property. This information will decrease your chance of making costly mistakes and will be invaluable whether purchasing rural, urban or waterfront property. It may be difficult to get answers to every question raised in this chapter, but you should make every effort to deal with as many as is practically possible.

23
Checking the Dwelling

Y ou have found the property that suits your needs perfectly. The view is magnificent. A stream runs through the property and the house is surrounded by beautiful mature trees.

But what about the condition of the house itself? A thorough check of the dwelling is mandatory if you want to avoid costly surprises at a later date.

If you have access, bring a flashlight and begin by inspecting the basement or cellar. This area will tell you whether or not the house is structurally sound. Large cracks in the foundation, irregular walls, and steel or wooden braces all indicate major structural faults. You are looking for a dry cellar or basement, but keep in mind that the time of year (the season) can affect this factor. A sump pump should be in place. Most basements have one as a precautionary measure against flooding. The pump is located on the floor in a dug hole which is below the footing's surface. When water reaches a certain level, it activates the pump and the accumulating water is pumped out to a drainage ditch or some other outside area. Some homes may have two pumps depending on the size of the basement and/or the chances of water seeping in. If a water problem exists, it may be due to poor drainage or poor construction. Many such problems can be corrected by having drainage ditches dug on the outside of the foundation, by repairing the foundation where cracks are occurring or by installing a mission gutter system to carry the roof water away from the foundation walls.

While in the basement, check the electrical system. Is it antiquated? That is, does it provide a service of 50 amps or less? If so, you may have to upgrade to 125 or even a 200 amp service, depending on how many electrical items you intend to bring and use in the house. You may want to consult an electrician on this matter.

Also check the heating system. You will want to know what type of system is used and how old it is. You can try to ascertain what the annual heating costs are by calling the oil or gas company.

For farm properties, having a separate door from the cellar or basement that lets you go outdoors without going through the main house is a great asset. Heavy tools, tables, and machinery may be easily stored in the cellar if such a door exists.

Be sure to examine all supporting beams for signs of weakness, rot, and insect damage. If the beams are full of tiny holes and covered with shavings, then you know you have a problem. Such a problem can be solved provided the damage is not too advanced. A good pest controller will answer many questions you might have in this area.

Moving upstairs, direct your attention to any water marks or discoloration on the walls and ceilings for this could be indicative of a leaky roof. Again, look for serious cracking on the top of door frames and around windows. Do all doors close properly? Do windows open and close freely and do floors appear level and solid? Turn on the faucets in the kitchen and bathrooms and flush the toilets to get some indication as to the amount of water pressure, the colour and odour of the water, and the efficiency of the drainage system.

Inspect the attic to determine the amount and type of insulation. While there, try to ascertain if the roof leaks.

Check the condition of the fireplace. With your flashlight look up the flue. Are any obstructions present? If the front of the fireplace has been darkened by escaping smoke, this may indicate problems with the downdraft or faulty construction of the chimney.

Check the outside of the house for storm windows and/or screens. Extensive peeling of paint and rotting of the sills may indicate a moisture problem. Check the condition of the porch and steps. If you can get on the roof examine the chimney for cracking and the shingles for wear.

If you are not experienced at assessing the structural merits and deficiencies of an older home, we suggest that you engage the services of a reputable, disinterested local contractor to review the entire residence before you make a purchase. This person will generally provide you with a complete written assessment of all aspects of the house, barns, and other buildings and often will offer recommendations on how to address existing problems and give you an idea of the approximate cost involved. The fee charged will be well worth it if it saves you making a costly mistake.

## 24

Water

F| or most city dwellers, water is not a source of concern since it is freely available by simply turning on the water faucets. The municipality assumes the responsibility for providing this service to all residents.

Most rural areas are not serviced by a public water supply. Therefore, it is essential for you to know where the water is coming from and whether or not it is safe to drink. Each country property owner must provide for his own source of water. Usually water will come from a dug or drilled well, depending on the depth and presence of groundwater.

Bringing in a well requires the digging, casing, sealing, and installation of a pump. A problem will arise if electricity is not available. In this case you would require a generator to run the pump. This motor could run several hours a day causing considerable noise and pollution, not to mention operational and repair expenses.

The cost of well drilling is based on the depth of the well, the toughness of the earth, and the accessibility to the area. If you reach water before hitting rock, the price is usually cut in half. There is always a chance you will not hit water. A driller will seldom guarantee water. He will tell you his price per meter (or foot) and then he will drill till he hopefully hits water. It is possible that he won't hit water, in which case you'd be out a few thousand dollars. However, it is rare that water cannot be found anywhere on a property.

Water can be found either on the surface or underground. Surface waters include rivers, streams, creeks, lakes, ponds, bogs, marshes, springs, and cisterns. Water is trapped underground in two types of areas: in aquifers, which are loose water-bearing materials such as gravel, sand, and clay; or in consolidated water-bearing rocks, notably limestone, basalt, and sandstone. Surface water sources are usually excellent for irrigation, livestock, fire fighting, ponds, and other uses, but cannot be utilized for drinking.

Most well water in Canada comes from underground sources. Underground water, or groundwater is purer than surface water since it has been sifted through porous earth. Groundwater exists only in the area called the "zone of saturation". This is the area beneath the ground in which all the openings and pores in the soil, sand, gravel, and rock are filled with water. Digging a well involves drilling a hole into the zone of saturation, which allows the water to drain by gravity from the saturated earth into the well, where it is pumped to the surface, only to be replaced by other water flowing towards the well. The rate at which this new water moves into the well, the recharge rate, determines the amount of water that can be withdrawn at any one time.

If you have a well, you will want to take a water sample to the local or regional Health Unit to determine whether the water is safe for human consumption. It is recommended that you always get the basic water test done, no matter what the history of the drinking water is on the land. The family living there may have been drinking the water for fifty years, but pollution can occur virtually overnight. Polluted water can cause cholera, typhoid fever, infectious hepatitis, and possibly polio. The basic water test includes a fecal and coliform bacterial count, which reflects the amount of contamination from human or animal excrement. If you want a more complete mineral and bacterial analysis (or to check for lead or mercury), you will have to pay to have it done by a commercial laboratory. If contamination of the water supply occurs, it is frequently due to the fact that the septic tank is located too close to the well.

If the water flows through farmland or irrigated land, it should be tested for the presence of pesticides.

The quality of water is also affected by an excessive amount of calcium and magnesium which cause it to become hard. Try to work up a lather with a bar of soap and a dish of water. The harder the water, the less suds you'll get. Hard water is less desirable for washing, cooking, and heating, but is generally not a serious problem. Water-softening equipment can be purchased and installed at any time.

Other minerals can affect the quality and taste of water. For example: iron in water affects the flavour of cooked vegetables, coffee, and tea. It stains clothes and water pipes and causes a reddish-brown sediment or oily scum to appear on the surface. Hydrogen sulfide gas and sulfate give water a rotten-egg odour and taste, which you will find highly objectionable. The water may also have silt suspended in it, which gives it a muddy or cloudy appearance. These and other mineral problems can be corrected through the use of chlorination and filtration equipment.

25
Electricity

T oday most rural areas are serviced by major power companies. The degree of service varies from area to area. Cost of installations and usage may present difficulties and it is vital that you be fully aware of the status of power for the area in which you have decided to buy.

If you are purchasing an older home, determine whether the present electrical service is capable of handling additional loads, such as more appliances, power tools and equipment. Wiring in many older places is totally inadequate. A new, heavier service, combined with new wiring and outlets is expensive.

If power is not presently available to the site, the utility company in many rural areas will bring the power to your location free of charge, providing it does not exceed a certain distance from the main source of power. If you are quite a distance from a central power source, you may be surprised at the cost charged for this service.

26

Sewage System

I f you are building or renovating a home in a rural area, you may need to add or upgrade the sewage system. This system normally consists of a septic tank connected to what is called a tile bed. A tile bed is a series of small trenches leading away from the house and a septic tank. The trenches contain special drain tiles spaced apart to allow seepage. In this way, the bacteria and waste are filtered through normal ground action.

If, however, the soil and ground condition in your area do not permit the proper amount of seepage, or what is actually called percolation, the local or municipal health authorities will refuse a building permit. Your municipal health department can give you some basic directions on how to do a percolation test yourself. If necessary, you can have such a test done by a civil engineer.

If you are putting in a septic system, you should keep in mind that it should be as far away as possible from buildings and sub-ground structures such as swimming pools and basements, and it should not be located in an area where the ground water will come to the surface during one season of the year.

## 27

Soil Content

I f you are planning to farm, you will want land that has a highly fertile soil. A dark, thick topsoil, rich in humus indicates high fertility. Topsoil is the loose upper layer of the ground. Humus is decayed vegetable matter which is black in colour and rich in plant nutrients. Good land should have at least 25 to 35 centimeters (10 to 14 inches) of loose topsoil.

One of the best ways to determine the texture of the soil is to rub some in your hand and between your fingers. Try to feel it. Sand will be loose and gritty; clay is heavy and compact when dry and sticky and doughy when wet. It is usually gray or yellow. Loam (a mix of sand, clay, silt, and organic matter) is black and will crumble in your hand.

Take a look around. This will give you a good indication of the quality of the land. Is the whole area hard and rocky? Is the growing vegetation plentiful and healthy? Better to see abundance than scarcity — you can always clear away the thick brush and weeds.

If the land slopes, be aware that plants will have a difficult time establishing roots because they tend to get swept away by the force of the water running downhill after a rainfall. Also keep in mind that sandy soils, steep slopes with little vegetation, and land that has been logged by the clear-cut method are particularly susceptible to erosion.

Drainage

In addition, you will want to determine the drainage characteristics of the land. Drainage refers to the amount of water that can be absorbed by the soil before it becomes saturated. Most vegetation will not grow where drainage is poor because plants drown when they are in more water than they can absorb.

If there is little growing on land that was once heavily farmed, something is not right. If possible, try to look at the land after a rainfall. Is the area flooded? Is water running off the surface without penetrating? If so, the drainage is bad. The subsoil might be unable to absorb much water.

You might try to test the soil under dry conditions. Dig four or more holes 10 to 30 centimeters in diameter and at least one meter deep at various locations on the land. How hard was it to dig? If the going is tough, you have an indication that the soil is bad. When you have finished digging, take a knife and scratch the sides of each hole. If dirt crumbles easily, good drainage should exist. If the soil is tightly compacted and hard to crumble, the soil is less than ideal.

Poor drainage often causes flooding in basements and septic tank systems. If your soil does not allow proper drainage, building and health inspectors will not permit you to construct a dwelling if the building codes require the installation of a septic tank with the house. If water does not drain properly, the water and sewage flushed into the septic tank and carried away by the tile bed will float to the surface of the ground during heavy rainfall. The soil must be deep and permeable to effectively absorb the effluent, or discharge, from the septic tank.

If you intend to have a septic tank and tile bed, you must be sure that groundwater level and bedrock are at least 1 to 1.5 meters below the intended tile bed.

Acidity and Alkalinity

Acidity or alkalinity of the soil is yet another factor which determines the quantity and type of vegetation that can be grown. These characteristics are measured on a pH scale which goes from 0 to 14, 0 being extremely acidic and 14 being extremely alkaline. A soil with a pH factor of 7.0 is neutral. Neutral soils are best for most fruits, vegetables, field crops, and flowers. Soil that is too acitic or too alkaline locks valuable nutrients into the soil, making them unavailable for plant use. An acitic soil requires an annual application of lime. An alkaline soil requires sulfur or gypsum.

It is possible to get your soil tested through government sources. In Ontario, testing can be done by the Ontario Soil Testing Laboratory of the University of Guelph, Department of Land Resource Science. This office also does testing for the Ontario Ministry of Agriculture and Food. Depending on the soil results, they will be able to tell you which crops will grow best on your land and, if problems or deficiencies exist, they will probably recommend chemicals or fertilizers to correct the condition.

If you are planning to build, remember that the best ground for this purpose

- has soil at least 1.5 meters deep

- allows good drainage of water

- does not lie under a high water table

- is level or moderately sloping. (Steep slopes are generally poor building sites because they can slide and erode.)

Your topographical map (see Section 11) will tell you a great deal about the lay of the land.

Working the Soil

D on't expect to purchase a farm and start making money. The capital required for raw land, buildings, equipment, and operating costs will more than surprise you. Often times, the cost of production is so far out of proportion to prices farmers obtain for their produce that it is ridiculous.

Families who have been operating a farm over the past three or four generations are far from living a life of luxury. This is true even when their farms are paid for and they do not have heavy mortgages and other debts.

The farmer's life is far from easy. In addition to all the normal every day problems the average farmer has to contend with, he must face the whims of nature which are completely uncontrollable and unpredictable.

Many farmers today are finding that their land is worth more for industrial development and recreational purposes than for farming. Thousands of small farms are being liquidated each year.

Zoning

$\boxed{Z}$ oning determines the location of homes, factories, parks, hospitals, schools, roads, sewers, and other essential services. A zoning by-law is the precise document used by a municipality to regulate the use of land. By-laws state exactly what land uses are currently permitted and provide detailed information as to:

– location of buildings or structures

– types of uses and dwellings permitted

– standards for lot sizes, parking requirements

– height of buildings, dimensions of side yards, setback from the street, etc. . . .

Each municipality draws up official plans setting out the general long-range policy framework for future land use. Zoning by-laws put those plans into effect and provide for their day-to-day administration. The zoning by-law contains very specific and legally enforceable regulations. Any new development or construction that fails to comply with a municipality's zoning by-law is not permitted and will be denied a building permit.

Most municipalities have a comprehensive zoning by-law that divides the entire municipality into land use zones. A detailed map of these zones forms an important part of the written by-law. Within each zone, the by-law specifies the permitted uses (eg. commercial, residential or seasonal) and the required standards (eg. location and size of buildings).

The basic types of zones are industrial, business, residential, agricultural, and seasonal. But there can be other types. Table 4-1 describes other common types of zones employed in determining land use. (Zoning symbols may vary between provinces.)

Table 4-1 Types of Zones

Zone Symbol	Description
R1, R2, R3, R3V	Dwellings, detached one family (Density varies in each of these zones
R4, R4V	Dwellings, semi-detached
R5, R5V, R5A, R5B, R5C	Dwellings, multiple, attached
R6A, R6B, R6C, R6D	Dwellings, apartment
R7	Mixed dwellings, multiple attached and apartment(s)
R1A	Residential special density zone
R1B	Dwellings, detached, one-family, condominium
RCL	Residential country lot
CN	Commercial neighbourhood - convenience store
CL	Commercial community - shopping place
CR	Commercial regional - shopping centre
CO	Commercial office
Ch	Commercial highway
CA	Commercial automotive
CMU	Commercial mixed use
MS	Industrial service
MP	Industrial park
MM	Industrial manufacturing
MX	Mineral extraction
PR	Parks and recreation
I	Institutional
Con	Conservation zone
A	Agriculture
ETC. . . .	

In addition to the division of municipal land into land-use zones, there are a number of additional specialized by-laws that can be used to control land use. For example:

- holding by-laws set out the future use of land or buildings but delay their development until, for example, local services such as sewers and water supplies are in place. Interim uses are usually specified. Before being able to use holding by-laws, municipalities must have appropriate official plan holding policies in place.

- interim control by-laws are used to place a temporary 'freeze' on certain land uses while a municipality is studying or reviewing its land use policies. Such a freeze can be put in place for a year at a time, to a maximum of two years only.

- temporary use by-laws zone land or buildings for a specific use for a maximum of three years at a time, with further extensions possible.

- increased height and density by-laws allow specific "bonuses" beyond the standards otherwise permitted, but apply only to developments that provide special facilities or services to the community at large, such as additional parkland or daycare facilities. Before being able to use these by-laws, municipalities must have appropriate official plan policies in place authorizing increases in height or density.

How Is a Zoning By-Law Passed?

When a municipality decides to prepare a comprehensive zoning by-law, it must first make adequate information available to the public. Local councils must hold at least one public meeting to allow citizens an opportunity to express their views before a decision is made. Notice of this meeting is given in advance, usually through local newspapers or by mail. Anyone present at the meeting has a right to address the proposal.

88

Local councils may also consult with interested agencies, boards, authorities or commissions before making a decision. When full consideration is given to all concerns, council may decide to pass, change or reject the proposed zoning by-law. If changes are made to the proposal, council must decide whether another public meeting is necessary.

Know the Zoning Laws Before You Purchase

You will have to do some research on your own to insure that the land you want to buy is located in an area that permits the specific activities you want and prohibits those you want to avoid.

A copy of the official plan and zoning regulations can be obtained from the municipal office. These documents will help you determine the direction of future development in that area. Do not assume that no zoning regulations apply just because the land is far away from a town or city. A piece of land can be very isolated yet still be zoned industrial. You might not be allowed to build a residence and could find yourself with a factory for a neighbour.

Zoning Restrictions to Be Aware of

- Most rural areas restrict the number of homes that can be built in an area.
- No home can be built on a parcel measuring less than the specified minimum area.
- Further subdividing may be prohibited.
- If the area is considered flood plain, you may not be allowed to build.
- Using trailers or mobile homes as dwellings is prohibited in some areas.

Do Your Homework

You should identify, locate, and visit all potentially problematic neighbours: garbage disposal areas, sewage depots, junk yards, quarries, etc.... These can present you with real frustrations even though they are located a quarter of a kilometer away. Active recreational centres, race-tracks, and amusement parks attract hordes of people, traffic, and noise.

Odors can also be a problem. Look out for creators of foul smells. Poorly managed dairy, poultry, horse, and swine farms can be unbearable as neighbours. Factories, lumber mills or farm processing mills are great for the economy, but not for your piece of mind. Local, town or village public works garages are useful except when the trucks start rolling past your bedroom window at 5 A.M. on a summer morning. Railroad tracks are great for transporting people and goods unless they cut behind your property line.

The above are mentioned in order to make you aware of the fact that you should spend a substantial amount of time investigating the surrounding countryside before you make any firm commitments. Talk to as many of the local country people as you can. They may be able to provide you with a great deal of information.

## 30

Land Severance

I f you are thinking of subdividing the property, you should be aware of the following facts.

A land severance is the authorized separation of a piece of land to form two new adjoining properties. This is commonly known as a "consent", and is required if you want to sell, mortgage, or lease a newly created parcel of land.

Therefore, to sever a piece of property you need a "consent" from the municipality. There are several reasons why you must obtain approval. The indiscriminate division of land, without anyone's approval, could have a long-term, negative impact on a community. It could, for example, result in overextension of municipal services, such as snow plowing, school busing, and garbage collection. Or it might result in damage to the natural environment if lots are too small to accommodate adequate sewage disposal systems.

Before you apply for a land severance, you should consult with municipal staff and/or the consent granting authority in your area. They will be able to tell you how to apply, what supporting material you must submit (e.g. sketches, plans) and if there are any special land severance requirements set out in the official plan.

Once you have applied, the approval authorities may give advance notice and information to anyone affected by your consent proposal. A copy of your application must be sent to certain municipal and provincial officials to give them an opportunity to review it and make their comments to the severance granting authority before a decision is made.

In considering each application for land severance, the approving body evaluates the merits of each proposal against such criteria as:

- the effects of the proposal on matters of provincial interest, such as the protection of prime agricultural lands
- general conformity with the official plan and compatibility with adjacent uses of land
- compliance with local zoning by-laws
- suitability of the land for the proposed purpose, including the size and shape of the lot(s) being created
- adequacy of vehicular access, water supply, sewage disposal
- the need to ensure protection from potential flooding.

When authorities rule on your application, they are required to send a notice of decision (approving or refusing the severance) to the applicant and to anyone else who has asked to be notified, within 10 days of the decision.

A severance approval will have certain conditions attached to it; these might include requirements for road widenings, parkland dedication, or a rezoning (or minor variance) to allow a new land use. In addition, the property owner may be required to enter into an agreement with the municipality to provide future services or facilities. Severance conditions must be fulfilled within one year.

When all the conditions have been met by the applicant, a certificate is issued by the authority and the severance goes into effect. Once a severance has been approved the new land parcels may be sold or resold without further approval.

If the transaction originally applied for (sale of property, transfer of property rights, etc.) is not carried out within two years of the date of the certificate, the severance is considered lapsed.

## 31

Other Factors to Consider

I f you are thinking of relocating to a rural area in order to escape the pressures, tensions, and problems of the city, you should consider the following factors before you make the move.

The cost of living may be lower, but you will have to sacrifice certain urban advantages such as higher salary and opportunities for advancement.

Furthermore, if you want to study or receive instruction on a part-time basis, you will be somewhat at a disadvantage in a country setting. If your children attend university, community college or a trade school on a full time basis, they will not be able to live at home and will need to pay boarding expenses. As well, you may not have cultural centres for music, art, and drama. If you presently enjoy an active social life, you must be prepared to make some changes.

When contemplating the purchase of a country property, be certain that you are aware of any potential future development and understand the consequences it may have on your property. If you are looking for a rapidly changing area, then there is no problem. If, on the other hand, you like the area as it is, you will not be too pleased with the changes resulting from rapid growth. The area in which you purchase may not be recognizable a few years later. If a land boom occurs, you may find an increase in taxes and a loss of peace and quiet.

Watch for ads promoting recreational lands or residential development in your area of interest. They are early indicators that change will follow.

Another factor you should consider is whether or not the population is declining. If it is, your property will decrease in value. You might have more difficulty finding employment or starting a small business and it may contribute to a lack of available services.

Statistics show that small towns with a population under 3000 are more likely to retain their rural characteristics, especially if they are a fair distance from major urban centres. Small towns close to major cities are experiencing phenomenal growth because, more and more, people are willing to spend time commuting in order to save on housing costs.

If you are thinking of starting a small business, be sure to consider whether the population base would support your venture and check to see if competition for your idea or product already exists. Talk to local business people, read the community newspaper and consult the yellow pages in order to see what businesses are already established. Do not forget to look at the local zoning by-laws and building codes.

You may wish to purchase a rural property and continue working in a large city. Take time to determine how long it would take you to commute to and from work, especially during peak traffic hours. While you may need thirty minutes to cover 10 kilometers and get out of the city, it is quite possible for you to cover another 20 kilometers in less than fifteen minutes. In larger centres, people are driving to the outside boundaries of the city, parking their car for the day, then using commuter trains or buses to avoid the on-going morning and afternoon traffic jams.

Electricity may have to be brought in if the property is isolated. How many of us can live without the conveniences of electric lights, television, modern appliances, power tools, etc.... Check out the cost of bringing power to the residence by consulting with the nearest electrical utility company.

If electricity is not available to the property, telephone lines are also likely to be non-existent. You will need to consult the telephone company regarding the charge for bringing in this service.

Check into road maintenance. A poorly maintained and infrequently plowed road can be the cause of a great deal of frustration. Notice how the roads look as you drive over them. Ask local residents about the quality and frequency of road work. You may have real problems getting to work if your road is left to the end of the day before it is cleared of snow.

What about medical facilities, shopping areas, opportunities for recreation, and schooling for your children? These should also be considered carefully.

If noise is something you are trying to escape, be aware that in the country sounds are greatly magnified. Will you be so near a road that you will be picking up the sound (sometimes the roar) of every vehicle that passes day or night? Heavy trucks can often run in the evening and on weekends. If you live on a steep grade, big trucks will be downshifting as they negotiate the hill. If you are located on the curve of a road you may be assaulted by the glare of headlights as each vehicle rounds the bend. On a mountaintop you will hear sounds from several kilometers away, whereas in a valley sounds will be muffled by the hills. Try to spend some time on or near the property and do nothing more than listen.

You must study, investigate, and review all the pros and cons. Only then will you be in a position to make a decision and feel comfortable with that decision.

32
Improving Your Purchase for Resale

I mproving property before putting it on the market can be done without spending a fortune. A few hundred dollars spent on the right improvements can often bring thousands more when you sell. Consider inexpensive things such as mowing, watering, and weeding the lawn. Painting and carpet cleaning also come high on the list. Scrub the walls and clean all windows, mirrors, and light fixtures. Consider adding little extras such as new lightswitch plates and a new shower curtain.

Going a little further, you might replace severely worn carpets, refinish a hardwood floor, plant new shrubs, and repaint the interior. Fix little problems, such as leaky faucets or torn screens.

Never overpersonalize the home as this can make it more difficult for the potential purchaser to visualize it as his or her own home. Re-painting the living room your favorite colour or putting up a favorite wallpaper may do little to attract a purchaser.

Do your best to recognize the weaknesses of your home. It is difficult to be objective about a place you have lived in for sometime. Ask others to share their first impressions of your home and point out any deficiencies. Start the inspection with a view from the road and work your way to the front of the dwelling. Record their observations and proceed inside doing the same with all areas of the house. Have them also point out those aspects of the home that pleased and/or displeased them the most. Never be offended by what they say, as that will inhibit honest feedback.

When preparing your home for resale, remember that colour will be one of the most influential elements of your presentation. It can also be one of the most cost-effective improvements. Colour affects our emotions and the way we perceive the size of objects. There are two important rules to follow with colour selection. First, keep it neutral. Secondly, err on the side of caution. The safe colours for walls are white and white tones such as bone, antique, cameo, and off-white. Popular colours such as blue, red, and green can be risky because they are either strongly liked or disliked.

Remember also that lighter, cooler colours contribute to an expensive airy feeling, while warmer dark colours cause a room to close in. A freshly painted interior creates a feeling of newness.

Use wallpaper with caution. Avoid loud patterns, including those with strong colours or designs and unusual textures. Everyone has a different taste in wallpaper.

Odd as it may seem, smell will also be a factor in attracting or repelling a potential buyer. Smells can bring back memories that are either positive or negative and can affect the buyer's attitude. Smells to avoid are cooking smells, smoking smells, pet smells, and medicinal smells. In addition, such smells as mildew, mustiness, oil or gas, septic tank, fireplace, and even wood rot suggest defects with the home. As was mentioned earlier, enlist the help of outsiders to detect such smells.

Pay special attention to the kitchen, for it will be one of the most important rooms in determining the sale of your home. While new appliances will create a favourable impression, it is not necessarily in your best interest to go out and purchase these simply for resale. Just make sure that what you have is in good working order and appears well maintained. Again, colour plays an important role. If a buyer walks into a home and sees the latest colours, he/she will presume the appliances are new. (It is possible to have appliances repainted by specialists.) Improvements to kitchen cabinets might range from installing new hardware on doors and drawers, repainting, recovering or refinishing the door and drawer fronts. You might even replace the kitchen cabinets entirely and redesign the kitchen. Don't forget to consider the countertop, the floors, and the lighting.

Bathrooms are another important selling point in your home. Make sure the bathroom smells clean and fresh and store all personal objects out of sight. If the tub and tiles appear worn, consider refinishing rather than replacing them. If the room looks small, the proper use of mirrors can significantly increase the feeling of size in the bathroom.

Do not neglect the basement and garage. They can reveal a great deal about the care of the home in general. In the basement, evidence of pests or rodents will almost certainly kill a sale. Keep the basement tidy and well organized.

Remember, a purchaser's first impression will be determined by the condition of the home's exterior. He/she will notice the colour and condition of the paint, the quality of lawn grass, health of shrubs and trees, type of light fixtures, and access to the front entrance.

Little things such as installing a door moulding and repainting the doorway, installing new front-door light fixtures, repainting a fence, planting flowers along the walkway, resealing the driveway, replacing dead grass – all contribute to a positive first impression.

When planning your improvements, always consider the law of diminishing returns. The money you put into fixing up a house will only increase the value to a certain point. After that, the dollars you invest will not be recovered when the time comes to sell. If you put $600 into some minor fix-ups, you may receive an extra $1000 when you resell. However, if you spend $10,000 on significant improvement projects, you may only see a $4,000 increase in the selling price.

You have a great deal of control over the asking price of your home and on how much time it will take to sell it. By making the right improvements, resale profits can greatly increase .

If you are planning to stay in the home for awhile and wish to do some major renovations, remember that remodelling or improving an older home involves a great deal more than simply what appears on the surface. The entire heating, plumbing, electrical and support system may be difficult to change without major unexpected costs. Many walls and ceilings in older homes have two or three layers of plaster which might make the cost of anticipated remodelling prohibitive. It is impossible to state a rule-of-thumb for building or remodelling costs because too many variables are at play – materials used, local labour rates, etc....

It is possible that soon after purchasing your new home and completing the improvements, an interested buyer might come along and make you an attractive offer. Before you set a price and agree to sell, you should consider the disadvantages of selling. Calculate how much of your money will go to taxes. Consider whether you would be lucky enough to find another place like this one. Would you have the time, the energy, and the money to make improvements on another property? You may decide that you will have a hard time finding a property that will increase in value more than the present one.

33
Using A Real Estate Agent

W hen selling your property, remember that there is no rule which stipulates that you must do so through a realtor. You can do it alone. However, there is a lot to be said for having someone else do the legwork. A good realtor will put up with all the paper work, will show the property, and will act as a go-between for you and the potential buyer.

In addition, because the real estate agent is constantly dealing with the buying and selling of property, he/she is in a very good position to advise you on a selling price. The agent also has ready access to prospective purchasers.

The biggest drawback to using a real estate agent is the commission charges. Depending on the value of the property, this can represent a significant amount of money. Often, owners will try to sell the property themselves in order to avoid paying the commission.

A real estate agent will generally not act for you unless you sign a *listing agreement*. This is a contract which entitles the agent to a commission. The property can be listed in one of three ways: multiple listing, exclusive listing, or open listing.

A multiple listing allows other agents to show the property, thus increasing the number of possible purchasers. This method of listing property ensures the greatest amount of exposure and is often the preferred method of selling if you are in a hurry.

An exclusive listing specifies the amount of commission to be paid to the agent and gives the agent exclusive right to sell your property for a specified period of time. It entitles the agent to a commission even if the property is sold by someone else during the period of agreement.

With an open listing, the rate of commission is usually lower than for an exclusive listing. The open listing allows you to enter into several listing agreements with other agents.

Real estate agents are paid a percentage of the final sale. The higher the selling price, the higher the commission. Therefore, it is advantageous for both agent and seller to obtain the highest possible price for the property. Nevertheless, since the agent does not earn any income until the property is sold, it is not uncommon for the agent to encourage the seller to accept a lower offer in order to complete the sale quicker. A smaller commission is better than no commission.

In selling a property, the vendor has the legal responsibility to disclose all information relevant to the title of the property. If the property has restrictions on title such as a right of way, an encroachment on a neighbouring property or an easement, these must be spelled out in the agreement. Minor deficiencies in the dwelling itself need not be reported (Ex: cracks in the drywall, leaky faucets, etc...). It is the buyer's responsibility to determine the extent of such minor flaws.

There are several ways of arranging for payment on completion of a sale. You can

- request a cash sale
- have the purchaser assume the existing mortgage and pay cash for the difference
- take back a mortgage from the purchaser
- have the purchaser assume the first mortgage and take back a second mortgage for the balance of the purchase price.

There are variations to these methods but those mentioned are the most common.

It is very important to remember that if you are taking back a mortgage, the terms of this mortgage need to be spelled out clearly in the agreement of purchase and sale. You need to specify the amount of the mortgage, the interest rate, the term, whether interest is compounded, installment periods, and whether or not any privileges are granted. (Ex: prepayment clauses, bonus payments on fixed dates, etc...).

## 34

Mortgages

W|hen buying property through a tax sale it is seldom possible to arrange for a mortgage beforehand. As a rule, you do not know if you will be the successful bidder, and with open auctions, you cannot predict the selling price of the property. Nevertheless, if you are successful in acquiring a property, you may wish to mortgage it at a later date. This might be done to free up funds for another purchase. Understanding mortgages will help you avoid costly mistakes should you decide to arrange for mortgage financing.

A mortgage is a loan of money from a lender to a purchaser. The purchaser (borrower) grants an interest in his/her property as security for the loan.

In order to fully understand mortgages it is important to define the following words.

Term: Term is the length of time the mortgage loan runs before principal and interest are due and payable. It is the length of time that the mortgagee (lender) will lend money to the mortgagor (purchaser). The end of the term is called the "maturity date". At maturity the borrower can pay off all or part of the mortgage and then renew with the lender for another term. Terms generally range from six months to five years. Short-term mortgages are preferred if you are planning to sell the property in a few years. Often a free and clear property (not encumbered by a mortgage) gives you more flexibility in completing the sale.

Amortization: Amortization period is the length of time it will take to pay off the mortgage if all agreed upon payments have been made. Amortization periods are almost always longer then the term. It is not uncommon to see mortgages with 5 year terms and a 25 or 30 year amortization period. Most mortgage payments consist of equal monthly installments consisting of both principal, interest, and often taxes. As payments progress each one contains a greater portion of principal than interest. Initially, payments are almost exclusively interest. As you approach the end of the amortization period, payments are predominantly principal.

Privileges: Rights are obtained when negotiating for the mortgage. The most common privilege is that of "prepayment". This privilege allows you to reduce the outstanding principal. With an "open mortgage" you can pay off all or part of the mortgage at specified times during the mortgage term. An example of a prepayment privilege would be one where you were allowed to pay 10% of the principal once a year and also increase your monthly payments once a year without incurring a penalty.

Another privilege would be the right of mortgage renewal at the end of the term. Without this right you may very well be required to pay the balance of the mortgage in full on the date of maturity.

It is also a privilege to be able to pass on the mortgage to someone else at the time of sale. Many mortgages require full payment when the property is sold. Others will allow a new purchaser to assume the mortgage only if the new buyer meets the lender's approval. It is important to remember that the person who signed the original mortgage continues to be liable for it even if it is sold, unless he/she obtains a written release from the mortgage holder. This makes it easier for the mortgage lender to approve transfer of the mortgage to another party. The lender knows that he/she can always go back against the original borrower if there is a problem. Such a procedure is well within the law and seldom happens since the value of the seized property usually exceeds the lender's losses should default occur.

Vendor Take-Back Mortgage: There are advantages that can accrue to both the buyer and the seller from vendor take-back mortgages. It frequently allows the property to be sold more quickly, as financing is rapidly available. A buyer can often secure a better mortgage rate and term than would be available through conventional lending institutions. In addition, special privileges can be negotiated. Often the downpayment may be lower than would otherwise be required. Delays, such as those that occur when going through financial institutions, are avoided.

One advantage, for the lender, is that the property becomes more saleable. You can structure the mortgage so that it is satisfactory to both the lender and borrower and you can do so in a short period of time. In addition, vendor take-back mortgages can be sold to another party if cash is needed – usually at a discount.

Where to Get Mortgage Funds:

As was mentioned earlier, funds can be obtained from the seller through a vendor take-back mortgage.

Traditionally, mortgage funds are obtained through institutions such as chartered banks, trust companies, credit unions, life insurance companies, mortgage loan companies, and even pension funds.

As well, it is possible to get mortgage money through private investors.

Borrowers will often go to a mortgage broker in order to obtain the funds needed. A broker will offer advice, search for competitive rates, and close the transaction. A broker usually represents a variety of institutions such as trust companies, finance companies, and banks. A broker can be very helpful to someone who does not know how to proceed in order to get the required funds. The broker will charge a fee, usually a percentage of the mortgage, for his/her services.

Institutional lenders require the filling in of detailed application forms and generally demand that an appraisal be done on the property. In addition, they request information on the borrower's credit rating and the security of his/her employment.

Institutional mortgage loans will generally not exceed 75% of the appraised value of the real estate. The advantage to institutional mortgages is that loans are not restricted to housing only. Many institutions will provide funds for commercial and industrial properties.

## 35

Waterfront Property

A cquiring a piece of waterfront property could be one of the best investments you will ever make. Looking at trends over the last several years, the demand for cottages and lakefront land has continued to climb and value has continued to grow.

Location

How far is the property from your principal place of residence? Travelling to and from a waterfront property located three or four hours away can become very tiring and discouraging, especially if you are planning weekend visits. And remember, the property will have greater value from a personal point of view and for future resale if you do not need to travel a long distance in order to get to it.

In addition to distance, you must consider the lay of the land. Is it situated high on a hill or on flat land? Is the property well treed or barren? What is the proximity to each neighbour?

The Property

You will want to look closely at the actual water frontage. Water frontage is the width of the property along the shoreline and, to a large extent, it determines the amount of privacy you will have. A 15 meter (50 feet) frontage can be very restricting and in fact, may not be sufficiently wide to allow the municipality to issue a building permit.

Be aware that over-development can cause a decrease in the value of the property and can impact negatively upon the environment. A larger population means closer neighbours, less privacy, and more unwanted and excessive noise.

Is the property located next to a road? Vehicles travelling on dirt or gravel roads can create a great deal of dust, particularly in warm dry weather. Try to determine the volume of traffic.

You may not want a property that is too elevated. Having to continuously climb in order to get supplies to your dwelling or to get to and from the shoreline will cause you to quickly lose interest. On the other hand, if the parcel of land is too low, it could be subject to flooding, thus creating access problems and possibly even septic system malfunctions.

Sun exposure is an important factor often overlooked by the purchaser. A property facing west will get sun from noon time on and will witness the sunset. As well, it will be exposed to prevailing westerly winds. If the property faces east, it will enjoy the sunrise but may lose sun exposure in the latter part of the day. It would also be exposed to fewer winds than a property facing west. Properties facing south receive the most sunshine throughout the day and the least amount of wind.

Access

With no access, the property will be of little value.

The best situation consists in having access by means of a public road which is maintained year round by the municipality. A privately maintained road can be a source of frustration if no committee exists to oversee the work and if the land owners refuse to contribute financially to its upkeep. The advantage of a private road is that area residents can better control the quantity of local traffic. If you are planning to use the property year round, you will want to be sure that snow plowing is done in the winter. In addition, watch for private roads that depend on a right of way over someone's property. You will need to ensure that legal access through the property will always be available.

As a rule, a property with public or deeded access is considered to be of greater value than one without any legal land access.

It is possible that the only access available is by water. If this is the case, the property will almost certainly ensure greater privacy and isolation and the price should be lower. Road access may become available in the not too distant future. You must consider carefully whether the prospect of loading and unloading your boat in all types of weather appeals to you. As well, is there a spot where you can leave your boat when not on the property or do you have to haul it by trailer back and forth from home. Do you have a suitable boat — one which will be safe and allow you to carry building supplies to the site? How will you manage if the boat breaks down?

Water

You will want to know more about the size and quality of the lake. Exploring the lake by boat will be your best means of evaluating it. An alternative is to acquire a good topographical map and study it carefully. Better still, do both. This is time well spent, as you are investing in the lake as much as you are in the property on the lake. The size of the body of water will affect your enjoyment of it. A small lake will provide limited opportunities for water sports, boating, and fishing, yet it may prove to be a much more peaceful environment. If fishing is to be a priority, you need to determine what type of fish inhabit the lake. You will also want an idea of fish quantities. The Ministry of Natural Resources can help you here. They keep detailed records regarding the type, quantity, and quality of fish in most lakes.

What about pollution? Consulting the Ministry of the Environment and those who are presently on the lake can help you determine the quality of the water. A great deal is heard about the harmful effects of acid rain and many lakes are now considered dead because of this phenomena. However, it is important to note that many other lakes are somewhat resistant to the effects of acid rain due to their high limestone content.

You may want to determine the degree of development on the lake. How much disruption has occurred along the shoreline? Have owners removed much of the vegetation and trees? Are there numerous man-made retaining walls and boat houses? They all impact on pollution, wildlife, and the fish population, as well as greatly interfere with the natural beauty of the lake.

Is the lake a feeder lake for a large waterway system? If it is, this may mean that the Ministry of Natural Resources will extract water from your lake to maintain water levels in other larger systems. This will cause the level of your lake water to increase or decrease, especially in the dry season. There are areas where lake water drops by as much as 3 meters and this could result in your dock, which once had water under it, now sitting on dry land.

Zoning

As with other property purchases, be sure you check zoning by-laws for the area. How can the land be used and what building restrictions exist? The area township or municipal office will be able to answer your questions. Some areas are zoned "environmental protection", which means that no building permit will be issued. Other areas are zoned "seasonal residential". This zoning may not allow you to live full time on that piece of property.

Municipalities have in place numerous regulations that impact on the size, location, and characteristics of the dwelling you plan to construct. You will require a certain amount of road and/or lake frontage in order to be granted a permit. The lot size will have to meet municipal standards. You will have to place the building at a certain distance from both the shoreline and the road. Regulations will also dictate the minimum and maximum size of your building and will restrict the number of buildings allowed on your property.

Septic System

If no septic system is presently in place, you will be required to obtain a septic system permit before being granted a building permit. The standard septic system consists of a septic tank which is in turn connected to a large tile bed. The system is usually placed behind your building and it must be a good distance away from any well. Close attention is paid to septic system installation. If not done properly, it can contribute to the pollution of lakes and rivers.

If you purchase a property with an existing septic system, be aware that it may need to be upgraded in order to meet current standards. The Ministry of the Environment can answer any questions you have regarding your septic system needs.

The Building

Some questions to ask include the following. How old are the structures? How is the main dwelling heated? Does it have inside plumbing? How many bedrooms does it have? What size of electrical service is provided? Is the building winterized? Is the roof in good repair? Is there a deck? There are many other questions that need to be asked. (See Section 23 for further points dealing with the condition of the dwelling.)

Utilities and Services

With most waterfront properties, water is drawn from the lake. You will need a water pump in order to bring water up to the dwelling. Wells are seldom found at seasonal residences. The lake water may be suitable for all of your needs except for drinking. Your drinking water may have to come from some other source.

What about electricity? If not presently running to the property, you will have to inquire from the local utility company regarding the cost of obtaining this service.

Is having a telephone considered a priority? Once again, you may need to inquire about the possibility of obtaining this service.

Get answers to questions dealing with garbage collection, police and fire protection, and the proximity of medical services. How close will you be to the nearest town and/or general store?

Miscellaneous

How much are the municipal taxes? Are there any easements running through the property (Ex: hydro)? You will be restricted from building within a certain distance of these easements.

Is there an active cottage owners' association on the lake? If there is, it is a good indication that owners are concerned about the quality of life on the lake. As well, the association is likely to sponsor a variety of social events such as regattas, sailing, picnics, etc.... These will all contribute to the enjoyment of your waterfront purchase.

If you are planning to buy a property near but not directly on a lake, a thorough investigation should be made to determine if you have legal access to swimming and docking facilities.

A Close Look at Tax Sale Procedures in Each Province

## 36

Tax Sale Procedures in Each Province

ONTARIO

W here any part of a municipality's property taxes are outstanding after a two year period for vacant land, and three years for improved land, the municipal treasurer may prepare a *tax arrears certificate* and register it in the appropriate Land Titles or Registry Office.

The *tax arrears certificate* (see Form 2 in the Appendix) indicates that the land described will be sold by public sale if the cancellation price is not paid to the municipality within one year of the registration of the tax arrears certificate. *Cancellation price* refers to an amount equal to all tax arrears owing, penalties, and interests, and all reasonable costs incurred by the municipality as a result of this procedure. Included in the costs are legal fees and disbursements, the costs of a survey, and advertising expenses.

If the cancellation price is paid, the treasurer must register a *tax arrears cancellation certificate*. Once this certificate is registered, the process is halted.

Ontario legislation does give permission to a municipality to enter into an agreement with the owner of the land which would allow for extending the time in which a tax arrear payment must be made. This agreement may set out such things as the number and amount of each installment required to be paid, but it cannot reduce the cancellation price nor prohibit any person from paying the cancellation price at any time.

In the event that the cancellation price still remains unpaid 280 days after the day of registration of the tax arrears certificate, the treasurer will be required to send a final notice. This notice is sent to the same parties who received the initial notice and again warns of the pending sale if the cancellation price is not paid before the expiry of the one year redemption period.

If the cancellation price continues to be unpaid, the treasurer must advertise that the property will be sold. Once advertised, these properties can be disposed of either by public auction or by public tender. At these sales, the minimum acceptable bid on a property is always the cancellation price.

A municipality may, if the council authorizes it, bid or tender on a property being offered for sale. The municipality must, however, have a municipal purpose for the property.

In Ontario, all tax sale listings are advertised using the same format. Advertisements are placed in the ONTARIO GAZETTE and also appear for four consecutive weeks in a major local newspaper servicing the municipality holding the sale. We have given an example of a tax sale notice held by public tender (see Sample 5-1) and one held by public auction (see Sample 1-1). While these property descriptions are fairly typical of all tax sale advertisements, slight variations may occur.

You will notice in the sample advertisements that notification is given regarding up to what point in time and where tenders will be received (if not an auction). This is followed by the time and place for the public opening of tenders or the holding of a public auction. Next, comes a legal description of the lands which are to be sold, along with a dollar figure representing the minimum tender amount or the minimum amount at which bidding can begin. A notice is given that tenders must be submitted according to a prescribed form (available from the municipality) and that tenders must be accompanied by a deposit in the form of a money order, bank draft, or certified cheque representing at least 20 per cent of the tender amount. A brief comment follows regarding the municipality's responsibility and a statement is made regarding what statutes and rules are governing the sale. Finally, the name of the contact person is given in the event that further information or a copy of the tender form is required.

Sale of Lands for Tax Arrears by Public Tender

Municipal Tax Sales Act, 1984

The Corporation of the Town of Parry Sound

Take notice that tenders are invited for the purchase of the land(s) described below and will be received until 3:00 p.m. local time on Wednesday, July 5th, 1989, at 52 Seguin Street, Parry Sound, Ontario, P2A 1B4.

Description of Land(s)	Minimum Tender Amount
Part of Lots 40 and 41, Plan 10 on the North side of Parry Sound Road and designated as Part 1 on 42R 4186 as described in Instrument number 75353	$1,911.34
Part 137, Part Block Y, in the Town of Parry Sound, William Street West side as described in Instrument No. 27808	$3,351.91
Part of Lot 27, Concession 1, formerly in the Township of McDougall now in the Town of Parry Sound, designated as Part 38 on PSR 1515 and being the whole of Parcel 18192 SS.............	$2,276.40
Part of Lot 8, Concession 1 of the Township of Burpee, in the District of Parry Sound, being designated as Part 17 of PSR 1132, and being the remainder of Parcel 121214 SS	$1,167.58
Lot 1 of Plan M 44, in the Unsurveyed Territory in the District of Parry Sound, and being the whole of Parcel 3739 NS	$ 925.16

Tenders must be submitted in the prescribed form and must be accompanied by a deposit in the form of a money order, a bank draft or cheque certified by a bank, trust company or Province of Ontario Savings Office payable to the municipality and representing at least 20 per cent of the tender amount.

The municipality makes no representation regarding the title to or any other matters relating to the land to be sold. Responsibility for ascertaining these matters rests with the potential purchasers.

This sale is governed by the Municipal Tax Sales Act, 1984, being chapter 48 of the Statutes of Ontario, 1984, and the Municipal Tax Sales Rules made under that Act. The successful purchaser will be required to pay the amount tendered plus accumulated taxes and the relevant land transfer tax. If a survey is required for registration of the deed the price of the survey will be the responsibility of the purchaser.

For further information regarding this sale and a copy of the prescribed form of tender contact:

Joan Sprunt
Tax Collector,
The Corporation of the Town of Parry Sound,
52 Seguin Street,
Parry Sound , Ontario
P2A 1B4
(705) 746-2101.

QUEBEC

T̲he disposal of tax arrear properties in the province of Quebec is governed by several acts. For most cities and towns, procedures for selling tax arrear properties are outlined in the *Loi sur les cités et villes*. (Large cities such as Montreal and Quebec refer to their city charter which modifies the procedures slightly.) For most other small municipalities throughout the province, the *Code municipal* outlines the regulations dealing with properties whose taxes are outstanding.

As with all other provinces, when property taxes go unpaid for a period of time, notices are sent requesting payment. If notices are not acted upon, steps are taken to sell the property at a tax sale. In larger cities, such as Montreal and Quebec, sales are handled by a sheriff. In smaller municipalities, it is the secretary treasurer who takes this responsibility.

By law, notice of tax sales must be placed in a local newspaper(s) in the area holding the sale and must also appear in the *Gazette officielle du Québec*. Copies of the gazette can be obtained by writing to

> Gazette officielle du Québec
> 1279 boulevard Charest ouest, 9e étage
> Québec, Q1N 4K7
> (418) 643-5150

The gazette is published weekly and tax sale notices appear in most issues. Listings are given in French only. The gazette can also be consulted free of charge at most public libraries (see Sample 5-2, Listing from the Gazette officielle du Québec).

For the city of Montreal, sales occur once a year – usually December 1st, or 2nd if the 1st falls on a Sunday. Notices of sales are placed in the city's two major newspapers. Sales are conducted by a sheriff and are held by public auction. The minimum bid required must cover the total of all taxes due plus incurred costs. This bid must also be for at least 25% of the assessed value of the property.

Ventes pour taxes, avis de publication

Communauté Régionale de l'Outaouais

Avis public est, par les présentes, donné par le sous-signé, secrétaire adjoint à la Communauté Régionale de l'Outaouais, que l'avis public de la liste des immeubles de la municipalité de Val-des-Monts, de la municipalité de La Pêche et de la corporation municipale de canton de Hull, Partie Ouest, a été publié au journal «Le Droit», les 29 et 30 octobre 1990, conformément à l'article 1027 du Code municipal; l'avis public de la liste des immeubles de la municipalité de l'Ange-Gardien et de la municipalité de Nortre-Dame-de-la-Salette à être vendus, le 3 décembre 1990, pour défaut de paiement des taxes a été publié au journal «Le Bulletin», les 19 et 26 octobre 1990, conformément à l'article 1027 du Code municipal; l'avis public de la liste des immeubles de la municipalité de Pontiac à être vendus, le 3 décembre 1990, pour défaut de paiement des taxes a été publié au journal «The Equity», les 21 et 28 octobre 1990, conformément à l'article 1027 du Code municipal.

Hull, le 2 novembre 1990.

Le secrétaire adjoint.
MICHEL PHARAND

Ville de Shawinigan

Avis est, par les présentes, donné qu'un avis de vente pour taxes pour la ville de Shawinigan a été publié deux fois en français au journal «L'Hebdo du Saint-Maurice», soit dans les éditions du 3 novembre et du 10 novembre 1990. Cet avis est accompagné de la liste des immeubles qui seront vendus, pour défaut de paiement de taxes, à l'hôtel de ville de Shawinigan à 9 h 30, le 26 novembre 1990.

Shawinigan, le 14 novembre 1990

Le greffier,
CLAUDETTE DOUCET

The successful bidder at a Montreal sale does not get title to the property until one year has passed. This one year redemption period occurs in order to give the former owner a final opportunity to pay all outstanding taxes and costs that have accumulated. Should redemption not occur within that one year period, the successful bidder receives clear title to the parcel in question (see Sample 5-3, Tax Sale for the City of Montreal). The list of properties in the Montreal sample has been shortened because the actual list took ten pages of space in the newspapers.

VILLE DE MONTREAL ❦

VENTE POUR TAXES	VILLE DE MONTREAL

Avis public est par les présentes donné, que les propriétés immobilières ci-après mentionnées et plus spécialement désignées dans une cédule déposée dans mon bureau, le premier jour d'octobre 1990; seront vendues par moi, à mon bureau dans la Ville de Montréal, le samedi premier jour de décembre 1990, à dix heures, à raison d'une réclamation de la ville de Montréal, pour taxes et contributions foncières annuelles ou spéciales.

Le shérif adjoint, Paul St-Martin

SALE FOR UNPAID TAXES	VILLE DE MONTREAL

Public notice is hereby given that the real estate properties listed hereunder and further designated in a schedule deposited at my office, on the first day of October 1990, will be sold by myself, at my office in the Ville de Montreal, on Saturday, first day of December 1990, at 10:00 a.m. on a claim by the Ville de Montreal for special or annual real estate or other taxes.

Deputy Sheriff, Paul St-Martin

No de compte	No	Rue	Cadastre subdivision	Division enregistrement	Nom du propriétaire	Montant capital réclamé
			9			
13065665	2174	DELISLE	138	4 QUARTIER SAINT-ANTOINE	M. LADOUCEUR JEAN	843.08
13072974	1605	NOTRE-DAME 0 7	2296	A02 QUARTIER SAINT-ANTOINE	MME LASCELLES JEANNE	1 727.66
				1		
				2		
				301		
13073550	1621-1677	NOTRE-DAME 0	469	8-1 QUARTIER SAINT-ANTOINE	5352 6362 QUEBEC INC	1 417.38
				7-1		
				6-1		
				5-2		
13087318	627	LUCIEN-L'ALLIER 206	2338	B10 QUARTIER SAINT-ANTOINE	MR BÉGIN LUC	4 623.71
				1		
				2		
				204		
13087382	528	LUCIEN-L'ALLIER A01	2338	A01 QUARTIER SAINT-ANTOINE	CONSTRUCTION LANTIER INC	195.20
				1		
				2		
14003831	317	PL D'YOUVILLE 35	231	A23 QUARTIER OUEST	M. JOLI RICHARD	2 026.24
				1		
				2		
				3		
				405		
14009228	216	DE L'HOPITAL 104	228	1 QUARTIER OUEST	121521 CANADA INC	1 440.41
				104		
				2		
22013200	1587-1591	PLESSIS	795	QUARTIER SAINTE-MARIE	M. SIMARD ALEC ET AL	4 853.97
22028425	1193-1196	DALCOURT	P366	QUARTIER SAINTE-MARIE	M MCFEE, RICHARD E	109.53
22028450	1127-1133	DALCOURT	P366	QUARTIER SAINTE-MARIE	M MCFEE, RICHARD E	1 789.38
22033778	1877	BL RENE-LEVESQUE E	1676	1 QUARTIER SAINTE-MARIE	R. LAGAULT PIERRE ET AL	443.85
				2		
				384		
22037908	1210-1223	CARTIER	443	P2-2 QUARTIER SAINTE-MARIE	J. CANNING STANISLAS	258.75
				P3-2		
				2-1		
				3-3		
22037100	1295-1303	CARTIER	443	4-3 QUARTIER SAINTE-MARIE	J. CANNING STANISLAS	2 159.97
				3-P2		
				3-1		
22053110	1421-1425	DE MAISONNEUVE EST	792	1 QUARTIER SAINTE-MARIE	M. SIMARD ALEC ET AL	176.23
22854992	1807	DE MAISONNEUVE EST	1696	R01 QUARTIER SAINTE-MARIE	INVESTMENTS CANADA LTDD.	33 459.73
				1		
				2		

Procedures vary slightly for the city of Quebec. As with Montreal, sales are conducted by public auction and are handled by a sheriff. As well, notices of sale are placed in local newspapers and the *Gazette officielle du Québec*. For Quebec city tax sales, notices appear under the heading *Ventes par sheriff* and not *Ventes pour taxes*. Quebec city is the only municipality in the province of Quebec which gives clear title to the successful bidder on the day of the auction. There is no one year period whereby the former owner can redeem the property. Like Montreal, the minimum bid required at an auction must be for 25% of the assessed value of the property.

Sales which occur in other cities and towns, and in smaller municipalities, are held in a way similar to those of Montreal and/or Quebec. Differences exist in regards to the redemption period, which is two years for these smaller municipalities. The successful bidder can occupy the property purchased at the auction. However, this purchaser must wait two years before obtaining absolute title to the property.

Property tax sales are held at various times throughout the province. You should call the municipality in your area of interest in order to determine when they hold their tax sales. You can also become aware of upcoming sales by consulting the *Gazette officielle du Québec* or your local newspapers.

BRITISH COLUMBIA

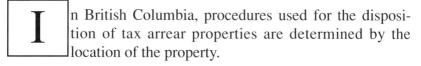 In British Columbia, procedures used for the disposition of tax arrear properties are determined by the location of the property.

– The *Vancouver Charter* governs the sale or properties in the city of Vancouver

– The *Municipal Act* governs the sale of tax arrear properties for organized municipalities (95% of B.C. citizens live in organized municipalities).

– The *Taxation (rural area) Act* governs sales in unorganized territories.

What follows is a detailed account of the procedures used in all three areas.

City of Vancouver

Tax sales for the city of Vancouver are held annually. The *Vancouver Charter* sets out that these sales are to be held on the first Wednesday in November for each even-numbered year and on the second Wednesday in November for each odd-numbered year. Sales take place at 10:00 a.m. in the City Hall. All properties whose taxes are outstanding for two years are auctioned at this time.

Notice of this annual sale is advertised in the month of October. Advertisements must be placed in three issues of a daily newspaper published in the city of Vancouver and in one issue of the *British Columbia Gazette*.

Though properties may be advertised, the delinquent taxpayer has until the day of sale to pay all outstanding taxes. If taxes are paid, the parcel in question is withdrawn from the sale.

All bidding at the auction must begin with the "upset price". This refers to the amount of taxes that are in arrears, interest on the taxes, and fees charged. The highest bidder is the successful purchaser. If there are no bids equal to or greater than the upset price, the city will be declared the purchaser.

The successful bidder must pay the upset price at the time of the sale. This money is kept by the city for one year – the time given to the former owner to redeem the property. If the property is not redeemed, the successful bidder receives title to the property. (See Sample 5-4, Advertisement for a City of Vancouver Tax Sale.)

You will notice in the Vancouver tax sale advertisement that the properties being sold are not listed in the advertisement. In order to determine what is being sold, you must report to the Property Tax Office. They will provide you with the assessment roll number and the address of the property. It is the bidder's responsibility to determine the characteristics of the property, to check for ease-ments and rights of way, etc....

Properties for Sale in Organized Municipalities

Sales of tax arrear properties in organized municipalities are governed by *The Municipal Act*. Ninety-five per cent of British Columbia properties are found in organized municipalities.

Sample 5-4   Advertisement for a City of Vancouver Tax Sale

CITY of VANCOUVER
SALE OF LAND FOR TAXES
WEDNESDAY, NOVEMBER 7, 1990

NOTICE is hereby given, that the Treasurer and Collector for the City of Vancouver is authorized and shall proceed to offer for sale by public auction at the City Hall, 453 West Twelfth Avenue, in the City of Vancouver, B.C., commencing at the hour of 10:00 o'clock in the forenoon of November 7, 1990, pursuant to the provisions of the "Vancouver Charter", each and every parcel of land and improvement thereon upon which taxes of local improvements or special assessments or other charges appearing on the real-property tax roll at that time have been delinquent for a period of two years, excepting such parcels are exempted from sale of taxes under the provision of the said "Vancouver Charter", and under any other law or statue applicable thereto.

NOTE: The transfers resulting from tax sale are subject to the PROPERTY PURCHASE TAX ACT (Proclaimed September 8, 1987)

ONLY CASH OR CERTIFIED CHEQUES ACCEPTED

Copies of the List of Properties to be offered for sale may be obtained (on October 31, 1990 after 12:00 noon) at The Property Tax Office, City Hall, 453 West Twelfth Avenue, Vancouver, B.C. V5Y 1V4.

LIST SUBJECT TO ALTERATION

DELINQUENT TAXPAYERS ARE REMINDED THAT A SAVING IN COSTS MAY STILL BE EFFECTED BY MAKING PAYMENT PRIOR TO THE COMMENCEMENT OF THE SALE.

(Ms.) P.J. Bruin
City Treasurer & Collector

As with the city of Vancouver, if property taxes are not paid for a two year period, sale of the property(ies) will be held by public auction the following year. Once sold, the previous owner has a one year period to redeem the property

Sales are held on the same date each year for all organized municipalities. The time of sale is always in late September or early October. Sales take place at 10:00 a.m. in the Council Chamber of each municipality.

All bidding starts at the upset price (taxes in arrears, plus interest, and miscellaneous fees).

Notice of the time and place of the tax sale and the description and street address (if applicable) of the property subject to the tax sale will be published in not less than two issues of a newspaper circulating in the municipality. The last publication should appear 3 to 10 days before the date of the tax sale (see Sample 5-5, Organized Territory Tax Sale Notice).

Where there is no bid equal to or above the upset price, the municipality is declared the successful purchaser.

The successful bidder receives a "certificate of sale" which describes the property and states that the purchaser will receive indefeasible title one year from the date of sale, unless the property is redeemed. If the property is not redeemed within the one year period, title is registered in the name of the successful tax sale purchaser. The previous owner loses all rights and interests in the property.

Sales in Unorganized Territories

For unorganized territories (less than 5% of the province) tax sales follow the procedures outlined in the *Taxation (rural area) Act*. If after a two year period, taxes for these properties remain unpaid, the property gets forfeited to the Crown. Properties are not made available to the public through an annual auction sale. These lands often become available through the Crown Land Marketing Program. They are disposed of according to a "best use" policy. This means that the property can remain a Crown possession, can be leased, or can be sold. Crown land properties are offered for sale twice a year and are listed in a publication entitled the *Crown*

Land Marketing Catalogue. Properties listed here are not singled out as being formerly in tax arrears. They are simply listed along with other Crown land properties which are made available to the public. To get the latest listings of Crown land properties for sale, write to the following address and ask for the Crown Land Marketing Catalogue.

> Crown Publications Inc.
> 546 Yates Street
> Victoria, British Columbia
> V8W 1K8

Sample 5-5 Organized Territory Tax Sale Notice

City of Port Moody
Notice of Tax Sale

TAKE NOTICE that subject to the prior payment of delinquent taxes, the Collector of the City of Port Moody will offer for sale on October 1, 1990 at 10:00 A.M. in the Council Chamber at 125 KYLE STREET, Port Moody, B.C. the following properties:

1. Lot 35, Block 2. District Lot 202. Plan 55 LD37 Group One NWD
   1377 O'Connor Street
2. Parcel A, District Lot 226, & Lot 43, Section 17, Township 39, Exp Plan 9433, Except part subdivided by Plan 74671, Group One NWD
3. Bay #22, Block 19, District Lot 233, Plan 1145 LD37 Group One NWD
   #16-3977 Grand Trunk Rd.
4. Lot 631, District Lot 203, Plan 45159 LD37 Group One NWD
   667 Gayle Road
5. Lot C, District Lot 377, Plan 18885 Group One NWD
   1033 Viewmount Drive
6. Lot 736, District Lot 377, Plan 50102 LD37 Group One NWD
   29 Lanier Crescent

NOTE: The transfers resulting from Tax Sale are subject to the Property Purchase Tax Act.

ONLY CASH OR CERTIFIED CHEQUES WILL BE ACCEPTED.

E.L. Crighton
Collector

ALBERTA

I n Alberta, all municipal tax sales are governed by the *Tax Recovery Act*. When taxes have been outstanding for two consecutive years, local treasurers are required to notify the registered owner(s), caveators, holders of building liens, mortgages, and other encumberances, that the property will be sold by public auction if taxes due are not paid by a fixed date.

Every public auction must be advertised in one issue of the *Alberta Gazette* and must be published not less than forty days and not more than ninety days before the date of the sale. It should also be advertised in one issue of a newspaper which has general circulation in the municipality holding the sale and it should be published not less than ten days and not more than twenty days before the date of sale. A copy of the sale notice is also to be posted in the treasurer's office. Advertisements for public auctions must specify the place, day, and hour at which the auction will begin. The advertisement must also contain a brief description of the property (usually a legal description). (See Sample 5-6, Listing from the Alberta Gazette.)

As in many other provinces, there is a redemption period whereby the original owner can pay all outstanding taxes and redeem the property previously auctioned. If the property remains unredeemed, the successful bidder obtains clear title to the parcel in question.

MANITOBA

P rocedures for the disposal of tax arrear properties in the province of Manitoba are governed by the *City of Winnipeg Act* (for the city of Winnipeg) and the *Municipalities Act* for all other municipalities. While there are two acts that refer to procedures followed when disposing of tax arrear properties, both follow a similar pattern.

Sample 5-6 Listing from The Alberta Gazette

Public Sale of Land

(Tax Recovery Act)

CITY OF CAMROSE

Notice is hereby given that under the provisions of the Tax Recovery Act, the City of Camrose will offer for sale, by public auction, in City Hall, Camrose, Alberta on Friday, March 11, 1990 at 2 p.m., the following lands:

Lot	Block	Plan
11	3	2112 S
(C. of T. 802038386)		
21-23	48	4727 S
(C. of T. 772036357		
4	E	5262 AB
(C. of T. 782022004)		
20	F	6212 AB
(C. of T. 842009552)		
30	4	782-0519
(C. of T. 852029302A)		
(C. of T. 852029302)		
(C. of T. 842005015A)		

Each parcel will be offered for sale, subject to the approval of the Minister of Municipal Affairs, as to those parcels which any person resides, or of which any person is in actual occupation, and subject to a reserve bid and to the reservations and conditions contained in the existing certificate of title.

Terms: Cash.

Redemption may be effected by payment of all arrears of taxes and costs at any time prior to the sale.

Dated at Camrose, Alberta, December 27, 1989.

R.A. McKenzie, City Treasurer.

If a property's taxes are in arrears for two years, notice is placed in the *Manitoba Gazette*. This notice indicates that the land will be sold by public auction if the arrears are not paid by a given date (see Sample 5-7, Listing from the Manitoba Gazette).

It is important to note that notices often state that the municipality intends to exercise its prior right to become the purchaser of all lands listed in arrears. This means that the tax sale auction will not be open to the public. In such cases, the municipality acquires the listed property(ies) and places a "tax sale certifi-

125

Sample 5-7   Listing from The Manitoba Gazette

Rural Municipality of Harrison
Sale of Lands for Arrears of Taxes

By virtue of a warrant issued by the Reeve of the Rural Municipality of Harrison, in the province of Manitoba, under his hand and the corporate seal of the said Municipality, to me directed, and bearing the date of the 11th day of October, 1988, commanding me to levy on the several parcels of land hereinafter mentioned and described for the arrears of taxes due thereon with costs, I do hereby give notice that unless:

a) All taxes that have been in arrears of one year or more following the end of the year in respect of which they were imposed;

b) The proportion of costs chargeable thereon; and

c) Such additional amounts as penalties calculated at the rate of 1 1/4% per month for each additional month or portion thereof, following the day the lands were advertised for sale in the Manitoba Gazette are paid, I will on the 7th day of December, 1988, at the Municipal Office in Newdale, at the hour of two o'clock in the afternoon, proceed to sell by public auction the said lands for arrears of taxes and costs. It is Council's intention to exercise its prior right to become the tax purchaser of all lands listed below:

Description	Arrears	Costs	Total
SE Site Pt 28-16-19W CT 111772	$ 6.98	$10.00	$ 16.98
SE 4-16-20W CT212331	1,265.27	10.00	1,275.28
SW 4-16-20W CT212331	1,599.38	10.00	1,609.38
Lot 4, Blk 7, Plan 502 CT 138910	158.66	10.00	168.66
Lots 16/18, Blk 13, Plan 502 CT 177447	464.45	10.00	474.45
NE E1/2 3-18-19W Ex Rd 6562 & 4873 CT 193771	832.65	10.00	842.65
NE W1/2 3-18-19W Ex Rd 6562 & 4873 CT 118477	960.90	10.00	970.90
SW 3-18-19W CT 139055	1,007.85	10.00	1,017.85
SE S1/2 4-18-19W CT 139055	832.78	10.00	842.78
NW 7-18-20W Ex Lake 13 CT 168268	423.44	10.00	433.44
Lot 6, Blk 2, Plan 930 CT 160923	482.57	10.00	492.57

Dated at the Village of Newdale, in Manitoba, this 11 th day of October, 1988

Shelley Glenn,
Secretary-Treasurer,
R.M. of Harrison.

126

cate" on them. If after a year taxes still aren't paid – i.e. the property is still not redeemed – the municipality can apply for title. Once the municipality acquires title it may use the property for some municipal purpose, it may put it up for auction, or it may attempt to sell it at market value. (It is important to contact each municipality holding a sale in order to determine what it intends to do with its tax arrear properties.)

SASKATCHEWAN

T ax sales in Saskatchewan are governed by the *Tax Enforcement Act*. When a property is in arrears, the local treasurer publishes that fact in a local newspaper. If the taxes are not paid, the treasurer issues a tax lien against the property (see Sample 5-8, Tax Lien). The lien can be removed by paying the back taxes. If taxes are not paid within a specified period of time, the municipality concerned obtains title to the land. It can then sell these lands by either public auction or public tender. The minimum bid or tender accepted must be sufficient to cover outstanding taxes and costs.

The sale must appear in a newspaper published in or near the municipality in which the land is situated and where lands are in a town, village, rural municipality, or northern municipality, by notice posted in the treasurer's office. Saskatchewan tax sale advertisements do not appear in the provincial gazette (see Sample 5-9, Newspaper Advertisement for a Saskatchewan Tax Sale).

The municipality can also purchase the property by paying all outstanding taxes and other costs. If it keeps the parcel(s) in question, it must demonstrate that it plans to use it for a municipal purpose.

The successful bidder at a tax sale receives clear title to the property. Unlike many other provinces, once a property is sold at a tax sale, it cannot be redeemed by the former owner. All sales are final.

Sample 5-8 Tax Lien

SCHEDULE

Form A
(Section 10)
The Tax Enforcement Act
TAX LIEN

To the Registrar of Land Titles for   Land   Registration District:
    Take notice that all parcels of land specified herein are subject to a tax lien under *The Tax Enforcement Act.*

(Description of Lands)

Dated this   day of   , 9   .

    (Seal of the   Treasurer, Clerk, Administrator
    municipality)   or Collector of Taxes

Sample 5-9 Newspaper Advertisement of a Saskatchewan Tax Sale

NOTICE

The City of Saskatoon, under the provisions of the Tax Enforcement Act, offers the following residential lot, zoned R2 for sale by public tender.

ADDRESS	LOT	BLOCK	PLAN NO.	FRONTAGE
726 Second Street East	21	3	G177	7.62 M

Sealed bids for the purchase of the above lot will be received by the City Land Department up to 2:00 p.m. Central Standard Time, Tuesday, February 19, 1991.

The successful bidder may pay the full cash amount offered for the lot within thirty (30) days of notification of successful bid.

ALL BIDS MUST BE ACCOMPANIED BY A CERTIFIED CHEQUE OR BANK DRAFT IN THE AMOUNT OF 10% OF THE TENDERED PRICE.

The City of Saskatoon places a reserve bid of $12,700.00 on the lot, therefore, any bids for lesser amounts will not be considered. The highest or any bid not necessarily accepted. The reserve bid and all bids received shall be subject to 7% G.S.T.

For further information, please contact the City Land Department, City Hall at 975-3278,
City of Saskatoon
Land Department

City of
Saskatoon

128

NOVA SCOTIA

In Nova Scotia, the sale of tax arrear properties is governed by the *Nova Scotia Assessment Act*. Once a year, Nova Scotia municipalities advertise for sale private lands which are in arrears of property taxes for three or more years. It is a legal requirement that these sales be advertised at least thirty days (one insertion each week) prior to the sale and in daily or weekly newspapers published or circulating in the municipality concerned (see Sample 5-10, Newspaper Advertisement of a Nova Scotia Tax Sale). Properties do not get advertised in the Nova Scotia provincial gazette.

A list, date of the land auction sale, and description of each parcel can be obtained from the municipal clerk's office. These parcels of land are sold at public auctions to the highest bidder. Bids below the costs and taxes owing are not accepted. You or your personal representative must be present at the auction and be prepared to pay the price for the parcel on the day of the auction, in cash or certified cheque. The municipality will issue a deed to the successful bidder one year after the sale, if the previous owner has not paid costs, tax arrears, and interest in the interim.

To find out if there will be an upcoming tax sale in your area of interest, you will need to contact the municipality(ies) in that area. They can inform you about any upcoming sales.

NEW BRUNSWICK

New Brunswick and Prince Edward Island are the only provinces in Canada that handle the sale of tax arrear properties through central sources – The Provincial Department of Finance. The *Real Property Tax Act* is the legislation which outlines procedures for dealing with tax arrear properties.

When property taxes are delinquent for two years, a *Notice of Liability of Tax Sale* is sent to the assessed owner(s). If taxes are

MUNICIPALITY OF THE
COUNTY OF CAPE BRETON
TAX SALE
WEDNESDAY FEBRUARY 27, 1991.

Taxes, interest and costs owing (the amount advertised) to be paid at the time of
the Tax Sale by cash, money order or certified cheque from the Bank (will not be
accepted if not certified), balance of your bid to be paid within three (3) days
after the sale.

**Public notice is hereby given in accordance with the provisions of
Chapter 14, revised statutes of Nova Scotia, for the Year 1967, and Acts
and Amendments thereto, being the Assessment Act, the following
properties situated in the County of Cape Breton will be sold at Public
Auction in the Council Chambers Administration Building, 865 Grand
Lake Road, Sydney, Nova Scotia, on Wednesday, February 27th, 1991, at
the hour of 10 o'clock in the forenoon.**

2. District #2, Account #153700, Property #02218233, land only, situate at Little
   Pond Road, approximately 100' × 187', assessed in the name of Charles and
   Marie Jetson (last registered owner Robert McFadden, Jr.)
   Taxes, Interest and Costs owing   **$288.37**

3. District #3, Account #261350, Property #01275946, land only, situate off Tobin
   Road, approximately 50' × 100', assessed in the name of Mrs. Catherine
   Smithson.
   Taxes, Interest and Costs owing   **$310.13**

9. District #6, Account #559650, Property #00078815, land only, situate at Upper
   Leitches Creek, approximately 100 acres, assessed in the name of Jeff Bridges.
   Taxes, Interest and Costs owing   **$564.78**

11. District #7, Account #723005, Property #03145407, land only, situate at
    Frenchvale Road, approximately 80 acres, assessed in the name of K. Geoff
    McNeil (Heirs).
    Taxes, Interest and Costs owing   **$548.14**

12. District #7, Account #738044, Property #04907478, land only, situate at
    Frenchvale Road, approximately 46.5 acres, assessed in the name of Cicily R.
    Majors.
    Taxes, Interest and Costs owing   **$627.23**

**Further descriptions of these properties are available at the Tax Office,
First Floor, Administration Building, 865 Grand Lake Road, Sydney, Nova
Scotia.**

**MIKE MACKEIGAN
MANAGER OF REVENUE**

not paid within six months, a *Notice of Tax Sale* is subsequently sent. A tax sale can be held one month after this date.

Sales are held by public auction and bidding starts at the upset price (taxes owed and other charges). In New Brunswick, in order to protect the owner of the parcel in question, the upset price is not revealed until the day of the public auction.

While the administration of tax sales is coordinated by the Department of Finance in Fredericton, actual sales are handled by the Provincial Regional Revenue Offices. Regional offices can provide a great deal of information regarding the characteristics of properties to be sold in their area. Most enquiries regarding tax sales get directed to these offices. They can provide legal property descriptions, maps, etc....

Notice of tax sales appear in the *Royal Gazette* and in local newspapers (see Sample 5-11, Listing from the Royal Gazette). Notices of tax sales are placed in the Royal Gazette three times a year: February, June, and October. These notices usually appear in the Gazette on the second Wednesday before a tax sale. Sales are almost always held in the last week of the previously mentioned months. Notice of tax sales also appear in local newspapers two Wednesdays before the sale. They appear in the most popular newspapers of the county in question.

To subscribe to the Royal Gazette, or to purchase single issues listing upcoming tax sales, you can write to the following address:

Royal Gazette
Queen's Printer
P.O. Box 6000
Fredericton, N.B., E3B 5H1

By consulting the Royal Gazette you can also discover land sales that are held by the Department of Supply and Services. In addition, you will occasionally find a section entitled *Sheriffs Sales of Lands.*

The successful bidder at a tax sale must wait one year before obtaining clear title to the property. This gives the former owner a one year redemption period.

Sample 5-11 Listing from The Royal Gazette

Notice of Tax Sale / **Avis de Vente Pour non-paiement d'impôt**

There will be sold at public auction on the 23rd day of February, A.D. 1988 at 10:00 o'clock in the a.m. at the Provincial Regional Revenue Office located at Provincial Bldg., Broadway Street, in the town of Grand Falls in the county of Victoria and province of New Brunswick, the real properties listed hereunder:

Le 23 février 1988 à 10 heures, au bureau de perception provincial situé à l'Édifice provincial, rue Broadway dans la ville de Grand-Sault, comité de Victoria au Nouveau-Brunswick, seront vendus aux enchères les biens réels énumérés ci-dessous:

Assessed Owner/ Propriétaire imposé	Property Location/ Lieu du bien	Property Description/ Désignation du bien	Assessment & Tax Roll Information/ Référence au rôle d'évaluation et d'impôt		
			Year Année	Page Page	Property Account Number/ Numéro de compte des biens
Edward C. Cassista	264 Basin Street Town of Grand Falls 264, rue Basin Ville de Grand-Sault	House & Lot 169 Maison et lot 169	1987	602	00274510
Vinal Nicholsen	Nicholson Road Parish of Andover Chemin Nicholson Paroisse d'Andover	Vacant Lot Lot Vacant	1987	5391	00324357

For complete metes and bounds description of the real property refer to schedules posted at the Provincial Revenue Office.

The above real properties are to be sold for nonpayment of taxes in accordance with the provisions of Section 12, Real Property Tax Act. Terms of Sale: Cash (Canadian Funds) or cheque, supported by a letter of Guarantee from a Bank or other Financial Institution. The highest or any bid not necessarily accepted.

Dated in Fredericton this 19th day of January, 1988.

Glenn E. Kitchen
Provincial Tax Commissioner

Pour une description complète des bornes et limites des biens réels, consulter les listes affichées au bureau de preception provincial. Les biens réels susmentionnés seront vendus pour non-paiement d'impôt conformément aux dispositions de l'article 12 de la Loi sur l'impôt foncier. Conditions de vente: En espèces (devise canadienne) ou chèque appuyé d'une lettre de garantie d'une banque ou institution financière. Ni la plus haute ni l'une des soumissions ne sera forcément acceptée. Fait à Fredericton le 19 janvier 1988.

Le commissaire de l'impôt provincial,
Glenn E. Kitchen

NEWFOUNDLAND

T ax sales occur in the province of Newfoundland as well, but infrequently. There are three reasons for this. The first is due to the size of the population (a little over one half million) and the second is due to legislation which prohibits the selling of tax arrear properties that are owner occupied (i.e. someone is living on the property). A third reason is that municipalities have the power to turn off the water supply to any residence whose taxes are in arrears. This is a powerful weapon in securing the payment of taxes. In addition, the municipalities can apply to the courts in order to have a judgement attached to the taxpayer's wages.

When sales do occur for non owner-occupied properties, they are governed by the *Newfoundland Municipalities Act* and the *Conveyance Act.* (The cities of St. John, Mount Pearl, and Corner Brook also have legislation which determines how they are to deal with tax arrear properties.) Sales can take place when an owner is up to six years in arrears. These sales are usually held by public auction. At such sales, the minimum bid starts at the amount of taxes in arrears and any other associated costs. The successful bidder gets clear title to the property and, unlike some other provinces, the former owner is not entitled to a redemption period. All sales are final.

Often the municipality holding the sale reserves the right to acquire some or all of the tax arrear properties. This is usually done when it has a municipal purpose for the property or when there is no interest shown by bidders at a public auction.

Notices of tax sale auctions appear in local newspapers four weeks before any sale. An address is usually given, along with a legal description (see Sample 5-12, Newfoundland Notice of Tax Sale).

PRINCE EDWARD ISLAND

P rince Edward Island tax sales are governed by the *Real Property Tax Act*. All sales are coordinated through the Provincial Department of Finance in Charlottetown.

When a property is in arrears for over one year, the assessed owner receives a *Notice of Liablitiy of Tax Sale*. If the owner does not respond by paying all delinquent taxes, a *Notice of Tax Sale* is sent out stating that steps will be taken to sell the property at a tax sale if remedial action is not taken. When taxes continue to be outstanding, advertisements for a tax sale are placed in the Prince Edward Island *Royal Gazette* and in local newspapers (see Sample 5-13, Royal Gazette Tax Sale Notice). For information on single copies and subscription costs for the Royal Gazette, write to the following address.

Royal Gazette
Queen's Printer
P.O. Box 2000
Charlottetown, P.E.I., C1A 7N8

Tax sales are handled by county sheriffs and a provincial representative. They are held by public auction. The minimum bid is for the total of all taxes owed and any other costs incurred in trying to collect due taxes.

Sample 5-12 Newfoundland Notice of Tax Sale (Partial Listing)

IN THE MATTER OF The City of Corner Brook Act, 1985, Section 163

IN THE MATTER OF the conduct of a public auction to satisfy the lien for real property tax held by The Corner Brook City Council upon certain real properties located within the City of Corner Brook.

NOTICE OF SALE

TAKE NOTICE that under and by virtue of Section 163 of The City of Corner Brook Act, 1985 and The Conveyancing Act, R.S.N., 1970, c.63, as amended, the City of Corner Brook hereby gives notice of sale by public auction of the hereinafter described parcels of land which have been assessed to the hereinafter named persons.

TAKE FURTHER NOTICE that the sale by public auction shall be held at the offices of the Corner Brook City Council, City Hall, Corner Brook, Newfoundland at 2:00 o'clock in the afternoon on the 18th day of August, A.D., 1987.

TERMS OF SALE: The highest bidder to be the purchaser, with the highest bidder to pay twenty-five percent (25%) of the successful bid at the sale with the balance to be due upon deliver of a duly executed Deed of Conveyance from the Corner Brook City Council to the successful bidder. The Purchaser shall be responsible for reimbursement of the City for the cost of a survey prepared by a qualified Newfoundland Land Surveyor and this cost will be added to the purchase price and paid upon delivery of the said Deed of Conveyance.

The properties offered for sale are as follows:

ROLL NUMBER	ASSESSED NAME AND ADDRESS	TAXES IN ARREARS AND COSTS	DESCRIPTION OF PROPERTY
10979	Reid, Est of Shuchuck c/o Anita Rainford 67 Centennial Place Corner Brook A2C 3Y7	$1,134.23	5,000 square feet in and around 9 Clyde Road.
12314	Steinbach Construction Co. Ltd. c/o Mrs. Sarah Carruthers 367 Queen Street Stephenville, Nfld. A2N 6R3	$843.85	6 acres in and around Innis Road.
12795	James Peterson 199 Reid Street Corner Brook, Nfld. A2H 3P9	$810.48	5,000 square feet in and around Lundys Lane.
14971	Nfld. Brokerage c/o Peat Marwick Ltd. Suite 1001 Purdy's Wharf Tower Halifax, Nova Scotia B3J 3N2	$481.68	975 square feet in and around Acton Road.

DATED at Corner Brook, Newfoundland this 14th day of July, A.D., 1987

POOLE, ALTHOUSE, CLARKE, THOMPSON AND THOMAS

Solicitors for the Corner Brook, City Council
whose address for service is:

P.O. Box 812
Corner Brook, Newfoundland   A2H 6H7

NOTICE OF TAX SALE

There will be sold at public auction on Thursday, the 17th day of January, A.D. 1991, at 12:00 o'clock noon at or near the Court House at 42 Water Street, in Charlottetown, in the County of Queens, in the Province of Prince Edward Island, real property assessed in the name of the ESTATE OF GUY D. PRINCE, formerly of Agincourt, Ontario and situated at Pleasant Grove, in the County of Queens, aforesaid. The above property is more particularly described as follows:

ALL THAT PARCEL OF LAND situate, lying and being on Lot or Township No. 34, in Queens County, Prince Edward Island, bounded and described as follows, that is to say:

COMMENCING on the East side of the Friston Road and at the Southwest angle of land in the possession of Patrick Neil;

THENCE Easterly to land occupied by John Lamphier;

THENCE South to land in the occupation of Michael Curran;

THENCE Westerly to the road aforesaid;

THENCE North along the same to the place of commencement containing fifty (50) acres of land at little more or less agreeably to a plan showing the location of said land on the margin of these presents being the lands conveyed from the Provincial Treasurer of the Province of Prince Edward Island to William Ross, by Deed dated the 3rd day of February, A.D., 1943 and registered in the office of the Registrar of Deeds for Queens County on the 27th day of April, A.D., 1943 in Liber 105, Folio 815.

The lands herein intended to be described comprising fifty (50) acres of land a little more or less and being the lands currently assessed under the name of the Estate of Guy D. Prince as Provincial Parcel No. 141366 and is to be sold for non-payment of taxes in accordance with section 16 of the Real Property Tax Act R.S.P.E.I. 1988, Cap. R-5.

DATED at Charlottetown, this 20th day of December, A.D., 1990.

PHILIP MacDOUGALL
Deputy Minister of Finance
Province of Prince Edward Island

NOTICE OF TAX SALE

There will be sold at public auction of Thursday, the 22nd day of November, A.D. 1990, at 12:00 o'clock noon at or near the Court House at 42 Water Street, in Charlottetown, in the County of Queens, in the Province of Prince Edward Island, real property assessed in the name of ANDREW WILLIAMS, Crapaud R.R. #4, in the County of Queens, aforesaid, and situated at Westmoreland, in the County of Queens, aforesaid. The above property is more particularly described as follows:

ALL THAT PARCEL OF LAND situate, lying and being on Lot or Township No. 31, in Queens County, aforesaid, bounded and described as follows, that is to say:

BOUNDED on the West by the County Line Road.

ON the South by the Bancroft Road.

AND ON the East by land in possession of John Simmons.

AND ON the North by land in possession of the Estate of Charles O'Connor containing by estimation twenty-two and three-quarter acres of land a little more less.

The lands herein intended to be described comprising twenty-two and three-quarter acres of land a little more or less and being the land currently assessed under the name of Andrew Williams as Provincial Parcel No. 625321 and is to be sold for non-payment of taxes in accordance with Section 16 of the Real Property Tax Act R.S.P.E.I. 1988, Cap. R-5.

DATED at Charlottetown, this 6th day of November, A.D. 1990.

PHILIP MacDOUGALL
Deputy Minister of Finance
Province of Prince Edward Island

Other Non-Traditional Methods of Acquiring Real Estate

## 37

Sheriffs' Sales of Land

A section that often appears in most provincial gazettes and local newspapers and one that frequently gets confused with tax sale lands is the one entitled **SHERIFFS' SALES OF LANDS**. While a tax sale is held when an owner defaults on his property taxes, sheriffs' sales are held for defaulting on any debt. An example might best describe how a sheriff's sale works.

If you were to borrow a sum of money from a bank for a car, furniture, etc... and you stopped making payments, the bank might force you to a court of law in order to get a judgement against you. This action need not be taken only by a bank but could be taken by anyone (individual, business, etc...) who had lent you the money. If the judge rules in favor of the lender, this lender is now able to file a **WRIT OF SEIZURE AND SALE**. This action would take place in a sheriff's office. The writ allows the sheriff to seize any assets owned by the debtor and to subsequently liquidate these at an auction. When the asset seized is in the form of real estate, the property can be advertised in the provincial gazette under the heading **SHERIFFS' SALES OF LANDS** and a description of the parcel is also posted in the sheriff's office. Notice of Sale is also placed in local newspapers (see Sample 6-1).

These properties are sold through the auction process. At the sale, only the equity in the property is sold. If the debtor had a $100,000.00 property and a $65,000.00 mortgage, the successful bidder would get the property and the mortgage. He/She would assume responsibility for continuing payments on the mortgage. This differs from the tax sale procedures in that the successful bidder at a tax sale receives clear title, thus assuming

---

SHERIFF'S SALE

\UNDER AND BY VIRTUE of an execution issued out of the District Court of Ontario to me directed, against the lands and tenements of Albert Phillip O'Connor at the suit of Bernard Casselman, I have seized and taken in execution, the right, title, interest and equity of Albert Phillip O'Connor, in and to:

ALL AND SINGULAR that certain parcel or tract of land and premises situate as Unit 64-3 in the register for Section D-22. Township of Gloucester, Regional Municipality of Ottawa-Carleton and known as 36 Prescott Drive, Vars, Ontario.

ALL OF WHICH said right, title, interest and equity of redemption of the said Albert Phillip O'Connor in the said lands and tenements, I shall offer for sale by Public Auction, in my office, room 2039, Court House, 161 Elgin Street, Ottawa, Ontario on Thursday, October 25, 1990 at 11:00 a.m.

This sale is subject to cancellation up to the time of sale without any further notice.

TERMS: Cash or certified cheque. Deposit of 10% of bid price at the time of sale. Ten days to arrange financing. Delivery only upon payment in full.

No employee of the Ministry of the Attorney General may purchase any goods or chattels, lands or tenements exposed by a sheriff for sale under legal process, either directly or indirectly.

Dated at Ottawa this 18th day of September, 1990.

Carol O'Brien
Sheriff
Regional Municipality
of Ottawa-Carleton

---

no mortgage payments whatsoever. Proceeds from the sheriff's sale go to the lender, with extra monies, if such exist, going to the person in default.

Specifics Re Sheriffs' Sale of Lands

The sale of land does not take place unless notice of time and place of the sale has been

- mailed to the creditor or his solicitor and to the debtor at his last known address, at least thirty (30) days before the sale

- published in the provincial gazette once at least thirty (30) days before the sale and in a newspaper of general circulation in the place where the land is situated, once each week for two consecutive weeks, the last notice to be published not less than one (1) week nor more than three (3) weeks before the date of the sale

- posted in a conspicuous place in the sheriff's office for at least thirty (30) days.

The notice of sale sets out

- the short title of the proceeding

- the name of the debtor whose interest is to be sold

- the time and place of the intended sale

- a short description of the property to be sold.

Adjourned Sale

Where the sheriff considers it necessary in order to realize the best price that can be obtained, he/she may adjourn a sale to a later date with such further notice or advertisement as he considers necessary.

***Always call on the day of the sale to make sure the auction has not been cancelled.

Abortive Sales

Where the land remains unsold for want of buyers, the sheriff will notify the creditor of the time and place of the attempted sale and of any other relevant circumstances. The creditor may then instruct the sheriff to dispose of the land in such manner as the sheriff feels will bring the best price.

## 38

Surplus Federal
Crown Property

L ands held by Canada's federal government are usually required for specific operational or program purposes of the various federal departments.

If no longer required for those purposes, the lands (with and without buildings) are normally designated for disposal and offered first to other federal departments or agencies. If no interest is indicated at that level, the lands are usually offered to the provincial government and after that, to the local municipal government.

If no interest is expressed by those agencies and there are no other factors such as sale of adjoining owners, current occupants or community organizations, etc..., the surplus lands may be placed on the open market for disposal by public tender.

The public is generally made aware of surplus land sales by way of local and area newspaper advertising, posting on the premises, public notices as considered necessary under the circumstances, and by written notification to the interested parties. Look for newspaper headings entitled *Notice Of Public Tender.*

The regional offices of Public Works Canada, whose responsibility it is to dispose of surplus lands, maintain mailing lists of interested parties. In Ontario, anyone wishing to be placed on such a list can write to the following two addresses, advising of general and particular interests and requesting that his/her name be included on the mailing list.

1) <u>ONTARIO REGION</u> — (Ontario, except for National Capital Region)

Regional Manager
Real Estate Services
Public Works Canada
Ontario Region
4900 Yonge Street
Willowdale, Ontario
M2N 6A6

Attention: Chief, Acquisition and Disposal

2) NATIONAL CAPITAL REGION - (Parts of Eastern Ontario, north to North Bay, together with Temiscamingue, Pontiac and Gatineau Electoral Districts in Quebec).

Manager
Real Estate Services
Public Works Canada
National Capital Region
L'Esplanade Laurier
140 O'Connor Street
Ottawa, Ontario
K1A 0M3

Attention: Chief, Acquisition and Disposal

Should you be interested in federal land sales outside of the province of Ontario, you should make contact with the following addresses.

WESTERN REGION – (Manitoba, Saskatchewan, Alberta and Northwest Territories)

Regional Manager
Real Estate Services
Public Works Canada
Western Region
9925 - 109th Street
Edmonton, Alberta
T5K 2J8

Attention: Chief, Acquisition and Disposal

PACIFIC REGION – British Columbia and Yukon
Territories

Regional Manager
Real Estate Services
Public Works Canada
Pacific Region
1166 Alberni Street
Vancouver, British Columbia
V6E 3Z3

Attention: Chief, Acquisition and Disposal

ATLANTIC REGION – Nova Scotia, New Brunswick,
P.E.I. and Newfoundland

Regional Manager
Real Estate Services
Public Works Canada
AtlanticRegion
P.O. Box 2247
1190 Barrington Street
Halifax, Nova Scotia
B3J 3C9

Attention: Chief, Acquisition and Disposal

QUEBEC REGION – Quebec, except for the National
Capital Region

Regional Manager
Real Estate Services
Public Works Canada
Quebec Region
2001 University Street
Montreal, Quebec
H3A 1K3

Attention: Chief, Acquisition and Disposal

## 39

Real Estate Auctions

T ax sales are not the only source of auctioned real estate. While many properties sold at auctions are considered distressed properties, it is becoming more and more frequent to find good quality real estate being sold through the auction process. This is especially true when real estate markets take a downturn and owners have a difficult time selling their property. They are often prepared to use the auction process in order to quickly dispose of their real estate.

The advantage for the vendor is that he/she receives an unconditional offer which specifies closing on a fixed date. This unconditional offer, which is accompanied by a deposit, puts the vendor in a less tenuous position.

Real estate auction transactions are usually one of two types. One type is the *absolute auction* whereby the property sells without a minimum reserve bid to the highest bidder regardless of price. The other type of auction is the *subject to seller confirmation* where the seller has the right to refuse the top bid. Here the seller has set a bottom line reserve bid which is not disclosed to anyone but the auctioneer. The latter type of sale is less popular, as potential purchasers are reluctant to bid because they fear that the seller may have set an unrealistic minimum.

Auctioneers will usually provide potential purchasers with an opportunity to see the property beforehand by setting *open house* times a few days before the auction takes place. Often the auctioneer provides an information package which includes a description of the property and an offer to purchase form. This gives interested parties time to consult with a lawyer or to check out the status of the property.

At auction time, potential buyers register, show their nonrefundable downpayments, and sign a *terms and conditions* form.

Short breaks are often provided during the bidding process, to give bidders the time to gather their thoughts, seek advice, or make calculations.

Contracts are generally signed immediately following the sale and closing procedures follow the same course as for other real estate transactions.

Real estate auctions are generally listed under the Public Notices section of your newspaper. The following sample (Sample 6-2) was taken from a newspaper advertising real estate auctions. (PLEASE NOTE THAT THESE SALES HAVE TAKEN PLACE. THEY ARE BEING USED AS EXAMPLES ONLY.)

Sample 6-2 Newspaper Advertisement of Real Estate Auctions

Real Estate Auctions

Sat., May 12 at 10 A.M.,

offering a total of 6 valuable and attractive Kawartha properties featuring: #1, a winterized cottage on Burnt River; #2, Fenelon Falls commercial mini-golf & fast food business; #3, Fenelon Falls commercial zoned seasonal resort; #4 commercial lot; #5, two Lindsay homes on behalf of Stewart Blackhall Inc.

Real Estate #1, 5 bedroom winterized cottage or home on Burnt River, 92' waterfront x 149' depth, approx 1000 sq ft bungalow, Lot 1 Plan 417, Sommerville Twp, Victoria County.   Directions from Hwy 35 between Coboconk & Fenelon Falls, go E on Baddow Rd to Conc 3 Somerville. See signs.
REAL ESTATE #2: NOTE- selling time 11 A.M. - 36 Helen St., Fenelon Falls, Commercial Hwy 35A. Location - a mini putt & fast food business opportunity, selling a turn-key operation fully equipped to sell burgers, fries, dairy products & zoned C2 with endless potential and tourist exposure. Legal description - Lot 32, Reg Plan 100, Fenelon Falls, large lot, irregular size, 94'x231'x114"x231'.   NOTE: '89 statements & equipment list on request.

REAL ESTATE #3 NOTE: selling time 11:45 A.M.
Directions - follow Ellice St. to 104 Wychwood Cres.,
Fenelon Falls. Holiday Haven Resort zoned C31
Commercial featuring a 4 bedroom bungalow, large
renovated quanset hut & numerous cabins, presently
rented monthly & no lease, showing a good income.
This property is adjacent to a proposed subdivision and
has an excellent development potential, back lot from
Sturgeon Lake. Legal description - Plan 22 pt block C,
E & H RP57R3295, Pt 1, RP574659, Pt 2, Village of
Fenelon Falls, see signs.
REAL ESTATE #4: Sells at 12:30. A vacant
commercial lot adjacent to #3 on Wychwood Cres.,
Fenelon Falls. Lot size 78' frontage x 158'. See signs.
REAL ESTATE #5: Time 1:30 P.M. New 2 storey brick
& aluminum 3 bedroom home, 183 Orchard Pk Rd.
Directions - follow signs off Angelina St. S, lovely
modern home on large corner lot 49' x 122', numerous
options including 2 4pc baths, 1 2pc, large master
bedroom, fully carpeted throughout, thermal patio
doors, modern atmosphere, double car garage, gas
furnace & more.
REAL ESTATE #6: Selling at 2:15 P.M. 2 storey older
brick home on Riverview Rd., Lindsay fronting County
Rd 17 situated on large 3.2 acre parcel with possible
severence potential & zoning possibilities, 3 bedrooms,
4pc bath, recently sandblasted & renovated. With
location and size, this property shows excellent
potential, rented monthly, no lease. Legal description
Lot 62, Plan 44 Ops Twp. See signs.

NOTE all starting times. Terms 10% deposit day of
sale, balance in 30 days. Guaranteed clear titles. Must
be sold. Don't miss it. Surveys & literature available on
request. Preview on May 5 & 6 from Noon to 5 P.M. or
by appointment by calling (705) 887-1951 or

Calvin Mabee Auctions
R.R. #1, Lindsay
(705) 374-4800, 374-4435 or Car Phone (705) 749-7609

## 40

Crown Land

ost of the land in Canada still belongs to the govern-
M ment. In fact, less than 30% of Canada's land is under
private ownership. Crown land (also referred to as
"Public Land") is land that has either never been sold to anyone,
or land that has come back into Crown ownership through purchase or non-payment of taxes. Disposal of Crown land is handled by provincial governments.

Through government sources it is possible to obtain residential lots, cottage sites, farm lands, recreational properties, and
commercial or industrial sites.

Residential sites are available in some provinces. However,
the applicant must be prepared to construct a dwelling within 24
months of the purchase.

The largest single demand for Crown land is for cottage lots.
Each year, numerous lots are made available to the public. To
purchase a Crown cottage lot the applicant must be at least 18
years old, a Canadian citizen, and a resident of the province during the 12 months prior to the sale. The purchaser must also
erect a dwelling on the purchased property.

Substantial areas of Canada's Crown land are suitable for
agricultural purposes. Crown land may be available to an established farmer who requires additional acreage adjoining his
farm, or for a new farm providing the applicant can demonstrate
that he can establish and operate a viable farming business.

Commercial sites are available for such enterprises as service
stations, motels, industrial plants, tourist resorts, marinas,
airstrips, golf courses, or different types of manufacturing com-
plexes.

You can obtain a book which outlines the possibilities, procedures, and regulations involved in acquiring Crown lands. It tells you how to go about making a purchase and how to lease these lands. For more information write to: **Crown Land, Box 5380, Station F, Ottawa, Ontario, K2C 3J1.**

41
Foreclosure and Power of Sale

V ery few real estate transactions would take place were it not for the availability of mortgages. The mortgage is a contract in which one party agrees to lend money to another party who wishes to borrow this money. The "mortgagee" lends the money and the "mortgagor" borrows it. When a mortgagor defaults on the mortgage, the mortgagee has the right to act in order to recover current and potential future losses.

A mortgagor can default in several ways. The most obvious is by failing to make the required monthly payments. However, it is also possible to default by not paying property taxes, by not insuring the property, and by allowing the property to become run down, thus diminishing the value of the land and buildings.

Foreclosure proceedings will cause the mortgagor to lose the property. A lender must, however, take certain steps before initiating this action. He must send letters of reminder to the mortgagor in default. If this fails to bring about the necessary payments, he will then send a demand letter. Often this letter is sent by the lender's lawyer. The letter demands that the breach of agreement be rectified and that all previous and current payments be made, otherwise further legal action will be taken. It is here that most defaults are corrected and the mortgagor assumes his/her responsibilities.

Should payments still not be made, there are two popular methods of dealing with the problem: foreclosure and power of sale.

With *foreclosure*, the lender asks the courts to transfer legal title to the lender. Any equity built up in the property is transferred to the lender and the mortgagor receives nothing from the proceeds of the sale. By law, the court must give the mortgagor a period of time to allow for payment of arrears and costs. Foreclosures are usually long drawn-out procedures for most lenders and consequently "power of sale" has become the preferred route to follow when dealing with a mortgagor in default.

The *power of sale* is more efficient and less costly than the foreclosure procedure. After receiving a power of sale notice, the mortgagor has 35 days to pay off all arrears and costs. If he takes no action the lender will list the property with a real estate company.

There are always properties being sold by power of sale. However, the number of such sales increases dramatically during periods of recession, high unemployment, and failing businesses.

It is no easy task to discover properties sold by power of sale. Mortgage lenders are reluctant to advertise the property as part of a mortgage sale, as this tends to lower the price. Instead, they list it with a real estate company and request that it be advertised and marketed in the same way as any other property. While the real estate agent tries to secure a selling price close to market value, there inevitably exists some flexibility with price, as the mortgage lender really wants to dispose of the property.

By contacting several real estate agents you can determine which properties are being sold as power of sale. "Power of Sale" advertisements do appear on occasion in the classified section of your local newspaper (see Sample 6-3).

150

Power of sale in Brampton. House must be sold! 3 bdrm., dble. driveway, single gar., upgrades, beautiful home, vendor motivated! 1st come 1st serve. All offers taken. Small deposit req. Good financing avail. 844-1877

POWER OF SALE $88,500
2 bedroom with underground parking, one block to Billings Bridge plaza, only 3 years old. Michael Spence 774-1963

42
An Alternative Approach

I n the event that you want to be a bit more adventurous and would like to try to secure a piece of country property without paying the current market value, we suggest the following approach.

First, determine where you would like to make your purchase. Then, pay a visit to that area's tax office. Here you will find recorded information on every property within that township. Tax rolls (or assessment records) give names of the owners, the address, the size and the assessed value used for taxation purposes. Each piece of land is identified by a survey number (lot and concession, or plan number) which will help you find the property on the appropriate map.

These tax rolls are public records and are available for inspection. Because of the obvious value of these records you will not be allowed to take them from the building.

You can obtain a map of the township you are interested in by writing to one of the provincial map offices listed in the

Appendix. We suggest purchasing a topographical map and/or township maps, if the latter exist in your province.

Using this map, you can mark off the general area of land you wish to consider and also determine which of the properties you previously listed fall into this area.

You might first of all isolate the names of people who live out-of-country or province. The reason for this is that if you start by choosing someone who lives in that township, it is likely that he/she will call an established real estate firm to handle the sale of the land. The out-of-towner may not have such a local resource at his/her fingertips. After trying the out-of-towners you could work on the local owners.

Remember, however, that even if the owner lives away from the area, it doesn't necessarily mean that he/she is unfamiliar with the value of the land. He/she may be fully aware of its worth.

After you have discovered the names of the owners and the size and value of their properties, you can then proceed to the next step which is finding out who wants to sell his/her property.

Write a personal letter to each owner stating your interest and asking if there is an interest in selling the property. You could receive a positive response from an owner who is desirous of selling his/her property. You must be prepared to make an offer or decide whether or not the asking price represents a considerable saving over what is considered the market value of the property. If you did your homework you will already know what the place is currently worth.

If the asking price is substantially lower than the market value you may succeed in acquiring a property for a very reasonable price.

## Chapter Seven

Frequently
Asked
Questions

What happens to the property if there is no successful purchaser at a tax sale?

Should there be no interest in the property, or no one successfully bids on it, the piece in question becomes the property of the town, village, township, or municipality. The municipality can then do with it as it pleases. Most often, it is put on the market through a real estate company and is sold at market value.

If I am the successful bidder or have the highest tender, do I get clear title to the property?

In 95% or more of the sales the answer is yes. The only three exceptions that we are aware of are

1) easements or rights of way that run with the land,

2) any interest that the provincial or federal governments might have in the land, (extremely rare)

3) any interest or title acquired by adverse possession by abutting landowners before the registration of the tax deed or notice of vesting.

We suggest asking the municipality concerned whether the property you intend to bid on is affected by any of these. They should be able to tell you.

What is meant by a plan number?

Plan numbers usually refer to town registrations of smaller divisions of land. Information for lots which are on a registered plan map is available directly from the municipal office in each area.

Can the original owner ever redeem the property if I'm the successful purchaser?

The answer to this question depends on the province. In some provinces, such as Ontario, there is no opportunity to redeem.

The tax sale is final and the successful bidder or tenderer immediately gets clear title to the property. For many other provinces, there is indeed a redemption period. (See chapter 5 for the redemption policy followed by the province in which you are interested.

Where do I find out where and when tax sales will be held?

We know of three sources. The first is your local newspaper. The second is your provincial gazette. Please note that not all provinces list their tax arrear properties in the Gazette. (See section 5 for those provinces that do list.) Finally, we suggest telephoning your local town, village, etc. . . and simply asking them if they foresee having a sale sometime in the future.

How are tax sale properties disposed of?

These properties are disposed through public auctions or public tenders.

At a public auction, you simply show up on the announced date and, as at any other auction, you bid on any property you are interested in. As with tenders, the highest bidder is the successful purchaser of the property.

With public tenders, you essentially fill in a prescribed form on which you state how much you are prepared to pay for a particular piece of property. Your tender is then put in a sealed envelope, along with a percentage deposit of your tender amount, and brought or mailed to the municipality concerned. On a predetermined date your tender is opened and, if you are the highest bidder, you are the successful purchaser of the property.

Can one still purchase Crown land?

Yes, it is still possible to obtain Crown land in the form of residential lots, summer cottage sites, farm land, recreational lands, and commercial sites. Most of the land in Canada still belongs to the government. In fact, less than 30% of Canada's land is under private ownership. Disposal of all Crown land is handled by the provincial government.

You can obtain a book which outlines the possibilities, procedures, and regulations involved in purchasing or leasing these lands. Write to: Crown Land, P.O. Box 5380, Station F, Ottawa, Ontario, K3C 3J1

Is the new owner subject to any tax penalties if he/she sells the property bought at a tax sale?

Once you receive title to a property purchased at a tax sale, it is subject to the same tax rules as any other property you might own. If it is used as your principal residence and is sold, it is not subject to a capital gains tax. If it is not your principal residence and you don't qualify for an exemption, then you will indeed pay a capital gains tax on resale.

Can the municipality bid or tender on a tax sale property?

A municipality may, if the council by resolution authorizes it, bid or tender on a property being offered for sale. The municipality must, however, have a municipal purpose for the property if it does bid or tender.

Is there a Land Transfer Tax payable if one is the successful purchaser at a tax sale?

In most provinces if there is a sale of land and the municipality determines that there is a successful bidder or tenderer, this person cannot be considered the successful purchaser until the sale price and the land transfer tax owing on the sale price has been paid.

When a property is purchased and possession is granted, is the property owned outright? What happens to any existing mortgages?

The new owner of a tax sale property does not assume the mortgage if one exists. If a listed property has an existing mortgage it is treated as follows: the tax office sends at least two notices to the lender concerned; if the lender has not responded by the time of sale the property goes to the new owner and the mortgage is dismissed.

Appendices

Tax Sale Checklist

1) Consult local newspapers or your provincial gazette for notices about upcoming tax sales. Call the city, town, village, or township for the area that interests you and ask the clerk or treasurer if and when their municipality will be holding a sale. (Addresses and telephone numbers for each municipality are found in the CANADIAN ALMANAC and DIRECTORY – See Section 18.)

2) If the municipality has a mailing list, get your name on it.

3) Examine the list of properties.

4) Call the municipality holding the sale and ask if they have a package that further describes each property. If they do, have them send you a copy. Municipalities will often send a small location map, a legal description of each property, and if the sale is held by tender, a copy of the tendering form. Occasionally, you may also receive information on zoning, building requirements, and additional data which will help you assess the value of the property. Examine this information carefully.

5) If the municipality provides little information and you wish to learn more about each property, follow steps 6 to 10 on this checklist.

6) If available, consult an Historical Atlas (available at public libraries). This will help you determine the location of the property in the county. Photocopy the area as it appears on the historical map.

7) If available, obtain an up-to-date county map for the area you are interested in. Maps are available from each county clerk (for addresses consult the CANADIAN ALMANAC and DIRECTORY) and from some of the map offices listed in Appendix C.

8) Acquire a good topographical map of the area in question. You might even consider ordering an aerial photograph. (See Sections 11 and 12.)

9) If necessary, use the Land Titles or Registry Office. (See Section 14 and 15.)

10) Pay a visit to the municipality's assessment office. (See Section 17.)

11) Visit the property(ies) and estimate their value. (Consult Section 20 for elements to consider.)

12) If the sale is being held by public auction , be sure to come prepared. Know what you are bidding on and set a figure in your mind over which you will not bid. (See Section 22.)

13) If the sale is being done by public tender, submit your bid using the proper tender form. Include a deposit of at least 20% of your total bid price in the form of a money order, bank draft, or certified cheque. Insert both items in a sealed envelope marked "Tax Sale For ..." and send it to the municipality by mail or courier, assuring that it arrives by the date specified. (See Section 6 – Municipal Tax Sale Rules.)

Addresses of Provincial Gazettes Which Publish Notices of Tax Sales

The Ontario Gazette
5th floor
880 Bay Street
Toronto, Ontario
M7A 1N8
(414) 326-5310

Royal Gazette
Queen's Printer
P.O. Box 6000
Fredericton, New Brunswick
E3B 5H1
(506) 453-2520

The Manitoba Gazette
Statutory Publications
200 Vaughan Street
Winnipeg, Manitoba
R3C 1T5
(204) 945-3104

The British Columbia Gazette
Office of the Queen's Printer
506 Government Street
Victoria, British Columbia
V8V 2L7
(604) 386-4636

Royal Gazette
Queen's Printer
P.O. Box 2000
Charlottetown,
Prince Edward Island
C1A 7N8
(902) 368-5190

Gazette officielle du Quebec
1279 boulevard Charest ouest
9e étage
Quebec, Quebec
Q1N 4K7
(418) 643-1328

The Alberta Gazette
11510 Kingsway Avenue
Edmonton, Alberta
T5G 2Y5
(403) 427-4952

Mapping and Aerial Photography for Provinces and Jurisdictions

Alberta	MAPS Alberta Energy and Natural Resources Second Floor, North Petroleum Plaza 9945 - 108th Street Edmonton, Alta. T5K 2G6	Northwest Territories	Maps and Publications Institute of Sedimentary and Petroleum Geology 3303 - 33rd Street N Calgary, Alta. T2L 2A7
Saskatchewan	Central Survey and Mapping Agency Saskatchewan Supply and Services Second Floor, 2045 Broad Street Regina, Sask. S4P 3V7	Manitoba	Map Sales and Air Photo Library Surveys and Mapping Branch Department of Natural Resources 1007 Century Street Winnipeg, Man. R3H 0W3
Ontario	Public Information Centre Ministry of Natural Resources Room 1640, Whitney Block 99 Wellesley Street W. Toronto, Ont. M7A 1W3	Quebec	Cartography Service Department of Energy and Resources 1995 boulevard Charest ouest Quebec City, Que. G1N 4N9
New Brunswick	Crown Lands Branch Department of Natural Resources and Energy Box 6000 Fredericton, N.B. E3B 5H1	Nova Scotia	Nova Scotia Government Bookstore Box 637 Halifax, N.S. B3J 2Y3
Prince Edward Island	Land Registration Information Services Surveys and Mapping Branch 120 Water Street Summerside, P.E.I. C1N 1A9	Newfoundland	Department of Forestry Resources and Lands Howley Building Higgins Line St. John's, Nfld. A1C 5T7
Yukon	Map Sales Geological Survey of Canada 100 West Pender Street Vancouver, B.C. V6B 1R8	British Columbia	MAPS – B.C. Ministry of Crown Lands Surveys and Resource Mapping Branch Parliament Buildings Victoria, British Columbia V8V 1X5
Federal Air Photos	The National Air Photo Library 615 Booth Street Ottawa, Ont. K1A 0E9	Federal Maps, All Provinces	The Canada Map Office 615 Booth Street Ottawa, Ont. K1A 0E9

Tax Arrears Certificate

Form 2
Notice of Registration of
Tax Arrears Certificate
Municipal Tax Sales Act, 1984

STEP 1

The _____
Name of Municipality or Board

To:

STEP 2

Address:

STEP 3

1   A tax arrears certificate, a copy of which is attached, was registered on the _____ day of _____
19____, against the title to the land to which the certificate applies as instrument number _____.

2. If you are a person entitled under the *Municipal Tax Sales Act, 1984* to receive this notice and you pay the cancellation price, you will, if you are not the owner or the spouse of the owner of the land, have a lien on the land for the amount paid in priority over the interest of any other person to whom notice is sent under that act.

3. If, at the end of the one-year period following the date of the registration of the tax arrears certificate, the cancellation price remains upaid and there is no subsisting extension agreement, the land will be sold by public sale.

4. You may claim entitlement to a share in the proceeds of the sale of the land by applying to the District Court within one year of the payment into court by the Treasurer of the proceeds of sale minus the cancellation price.

5. If there is no successful purchaser at the public sale, the land, upon the registration of a notice of vesting will vest in the municipality *(or board)*.

STEP 4

6. *Inquiries related to the matters set out in this notice may be directed to:*

Title	Name of Municipality or Board

Address of Municipality or Board

STEP 5

STEP 6

Dated at   this   day of   19

STEP 7

....
Signature of Treasurer or Other Officer or Employee Authorized to Give this Notice   Title

Note: This document need not be registered.

165

Imperial-Metric Conversion Tables

LENGTHS AND DISTANCES

From miles	*to*	Kilometres	*multiply by*	1.6093
kilometres		miles		0.6214
feet		metres		0.3048
metres		feet		3.2808
kilometres		feet		3280.840
metres		inches		39.37
inches		centimetres		2.54
nautical miles		feet		6080.27

AREAS

From square miles	*to*	square kilometres	*multiply by*	2.5900
square feet		square metres		0.0929
acres		square feet		43,560
square miles		acres		640
square kilometres		square miles		0.3861
hectares		square metres		10,000
hectares		acres		2.47

VOLUMES

From cubic feet	*to*	imperial gallons	*multiply by*	6.24
cubic feet		cubic metres		0.0283
cubic metres		cubic feet		35.31
cubic miles		acre feet		3,379,200
cubic miles		cubic metres		4,168,260,100
Imperial gallons		litres		4.5460
American gallons		litres		3.7853
litres Imperial		gallons		0.2201

WEIGHT

From pounds	*to*	Kilograms	*multiply by*	0.4536
kilograms		pounds		2.2046

Ontario Land Registry Offices

No.	Office	Location	Telephone
01	Algoma Sault	Ste Marie	(705) 253-8887
02	Brant	Brantford	(519) 752-8321
03	Bruce	Walkerton	(519) 881-2259
04	Ottawa-Carleton	Ottawa	(613) 239-1230
05	Ottawa-Carleton	Ottawa	(613) 239-1319
06	Cochrane	Cochrane	(705) 272-5791
07	Dufferin	Orangeville	(519) 941-1481
08	Dundas	Morrisburg	(613) 543-2583
09	Port Hope	Port Hope	(416) 885-5616
10	Newcastle	Bowmanville	(416) 623-5386
11	Elgin	St. Thomas	(519) 631-3015
12	Essex	Windsor	(519) 254-6363
13	Frontenac	Kingston	(613) 548-6767
14	Glengarry	Alexandria	(613) 525-1315
15	Grenville	Prescott	(613) 925-3177
16	Grey North	Owen Sound	(519) 376-1637
17	Grey South	Durham	(519) 369-2011
18	Haldimand	Cayuga	(416) 772-3531
19	Haliburton	Minden	(705) 286-1391
20	Halton	Milton	(416) 878-7287
21	Hastings	Belleville	(613) 968-4597
22	Huron	Goderich	(519) 524-9562
23	Kenora	Kenora	(807) 468-3138
24	Kent	Chatham	(519) 352-5520
25	Lambton	Sarnia	(519) 337-2393
26	Lanark	North Almonte	(613) 256-1577
27	Lanark South	Perth	(613) 267-1144
28	Leeds	Brockville	(613) 345-5751

29	Lennox	Napanee	(613) 354-3751
30	Niagara North	St. Catharines	(416) 684-6351
31	Manitoulin	Gore Bay	(705) 282-2442
33	Middlesex East	London	(519) 679-7180
34	Middlesex West	Glencoe	(519) 287-2234
35	Muskoka	Bracebridge	(705) 645-4415
36	Nipissing	North Bay	(705) 474-2270
37	Norfolk	Simcoe	(519) 426-2216
38	Northumberland East	Colborne	(416) 355-2338
39	Northumberland West	Cobourg	(416) 372-3813
40	Durham	Oshawa	(416) 436-3521
41	Oxford	Woodstock	(519) 537-6287
42	Parry Sound	Parry Sound	(705) 746-5816
43	Peel	Brampton	(416) 457-5350
44	Perth	Stratford	(519) 271-3343
45	Peterborough	Peterborough	(705) 745-0583
46	Prescott	L'Orignal	(613) 675-4648
47	Prince Edward	Picton	(613) 476-3219
48	Rainy River	Fort Frances	(807) 274-5451
49	Renfrew	Pembroke	(613) 732-8331
50	Russell	Russell	(613) 445-2138
51	Simcoe	Barrie	(705) 734-2722
52	Stormont	Cornwall	(613) 932-4522
53	Sudbury	Sudbury	(705) 675-4300
54	Timiskaming	Haileybury	(705) 672-3332
55	Thunder Bay	Thunder Bay	(807) 475-1235
57	Victoria	Lindsay	(705) 324-4912
58	Waterloo North	Kitchener	(519) 576-1330
59	Niagara South	Welland	(416) 735-4011
60	Wellington North	Arthur	(519) 848-2300
61	Wellington South	Guelph	(519) 822-0251
62	Wentworth	Hamilton	(416) 521-7561
63	Toronto	Toronto	(416) 965-7553
64	Toronto Boroughs	Toronto	(416) 965-7588
65	York Region	Newmarket	(416) 895-1516
66	Metro Toronto	Toronto	(416) 965-5248
67	Waterloo South	Cambridge	(519) 653-5778

Glossary

Appraisal: A written estimate of the market value of a piece of property, generally made by a qualified expert.

Arrears: A debt that is due but not yet paid. Payments (e.g. rent, taxes or interest payments) that have not been made at the appointed time, i.e. on the due date. A sum of money that is in arrears remains in arrears until there is a proper payment.

Assessed tenants in occupation of the land: Assessed tenants in occupation of the land are those persons whose names appear on the last returned assessment roll, or those appearing in the records of the land registry office as assessed tenants.

Assessed value: This is the value of a piece of property set by a municipality for taxation purposes.

Auction: Auction may be defined as a public sale of an item to the highest bidder. Auction selling is a competitive bidding method where all prospective and interested buyers can bid and have equal access to the supply of the commodity being offered for sale. In auctions where many buyers participate, this method provides the best chance that the commodity being offered for sale receives the highest possible price under the existing market conditions.

Building codes: Regulations established by local governments which outline building requirements for particular areas and types of structures.

Cancellation price: This is an amount equal to all the tax arrears owing, plus all current real property taxes owing, penalties and interest, and all reasonable costs incurred by the municipality after the treasurer becomes entitled to register a tax arrears certificate. Included in the cost of proceeding under the Act are legal fees and disbursements, the costs of a survey, the costs of preparing and registering an extension agreement, and advertising expenses.

Caveat emptor: 'Let the buyer beware'. A general principle of English common law that a buyer of goods should make all reasonable enquiries before effecting a purchase. "Caveat emptor" in Latin or law does not mean that a buyer must take a chance, it means he must take care.

Certificate of title: Acknowledgement by a government that the title deed has been registered in a Registry or Land Titles office.

Chain of title: A history of the conveyances and encumbrances affecting a title from the time the original title was granted or as far back as records are available.

Chattels: These are moveable possessions such as furniture, etc.... A hot water tank before it is installed is a moveable possession. Once installed, it is not.

Chief Administrative Officer: Is the senior staff member of a municipality. Many municipal councils have appointed such a person, usually called the 'CAO' or some variation such as 'manager', 'clerk-administrator' or 'clerk-controller'. In smaller municipalities, this individual will often hold another staff position as well as being responsible for administration.

Clerk: Is the member of staff whose major duties are to record all resolutions, decisions, and other proceedings of the council, and to keep its books, records, accounts, and other documents. Every council is required to appoint a clerk.

Cloud on title: Consists of an outstanding claim which if proven to be accurate, would affect a current owner's title.

Conveyance: The transfer of a land title from one party to another.

County: Is a municipality which is a federation of the towns, villages, and townships within its boundaries. Each of the participating local municipalities in the county has an elected council, and designated members of all of these councils combine to form the county council. The county is responsible for a limited number of functions, with major roads being the most important one. Local councils are responsible for the majority of municipal functions.

Cities and separated towns, even though geographically part of the county, do not participate in the county political system. The councils of these local municipalities are responsible for most municipal functions within their boundaries.

County geographical boundaries are used for judicial and a number of administrative purposes.

Deed: A written, sealed instrument of bond, contract or transfer.

Deed restriction: A restriction on the deed which would limit the use of the land. This might affect the size, type, value, or placement of improvements that might be placed on the property.

Delinquent loan or payment: A sum of money that is unpaid when due either under the terms of a contract (e.g. rent or mortgage interest) , or by law (e.g. a tax) . A payment that has fallen into arrears.

District town: Is the main location in a territorial district of the Province's legal and judicial systems, including facilities for the courts, Sheriff, Crown Attorney, personal property, and land registration, property assessment, and related activities. "District town" is not a legal or municipal designation and is not necessarily either a town or the largest urban centre in the district.

Easement: The right someone has to use property owned by another. An easement can be written into a deed or occur through long use.

Encroachment: Unlawful trespassing on another individual's property often caused by a building, or part of a building.

Encumbrance: This refers to any legal claim registered against a property. (EX: a mortgage)

Espenses: Any documentable costs incurred by the municipality against the property during the tax recovery process.

Foreclosure: The taking of legal action against the mortgagor and property owner for breach of mortgage covenants on the property. This usually results once substantial arrears have occurred in mortgage payments and is considered a step of last resort.

Grant: This is an instrument of conveyance which transfers property from one to another.

Grantee: The buyer.

Grantor: The seller.

Improved land: This is land which is liable to be separately assessed, and which has a building on it. Land which is in actual agricultural use is also considered improved, whether or not it has any buildings on it.

Improvement district: This is a municipality. Its powers are exercised by a board of trustees. The actions of the trustees are subject to Provincial supervision. This type of municipality has been established in previously unsettled or sparsely settled areas, without municipal organization, where a new resource industry located and municipal government was required immediately. Once a new resource community becomes more established, the improvement district is usually replaced by a conventional local municipality.

Instrument: A piece of writing instructing one in regard to something that has been agreed on.

Lease: A contract under which the lessor is obliged to give the lessee the enjoyment and use of a thing for a certain time, in return for rent.

Lien: A legal claim affecting a property.

Local municipality: Means a city, town, village, or township.

Market value: This is generally referred to as the highest price which a property will bring if put for sale on the open market.

Mechanic's lien: A lien filed and registered against property by a person or corporate body, for labour and/or materials supplied for the improvement of the property.

Mineral rights: A right given to one to remove, mine, or explore various subterranean minerals or deposits. This does not always give the owner of the mineral rights title to the property itself.

Mortgage: A pledge or security of a particular property for the payment of a debt or the performance of some other obligation.

Mortgagee: One who lends money to a mortgagor.

Mortgagor: One who borrows money against real estate as his security.

Municipality: Is an area whose inhabitants are incorporated. Its powers, except in the case of an improvement district, are exercised by a council composed of individuals elected by the electors of the municipality.

Occupied Property: Land is considered occupied when used as a residence, place of business, being cropped, grazed, fallowed, logged or reserved for hay.

Open mortgage: A mortgage that may be prepaid, with or without penalty, prior to the expiration of its term.

Option: A right or a consideration to purchase or lease a property upon specified terms within a specified time. If the right is not exercised, the option holder is not subject to liability for damages. If exercised, the grantor of option must perform.

Parcel: Means land that is:

(i)   a lot or block in a registered subdivision or a quarter section or any part of such lot, block or quarter section;

(ii)   a number of lots, blocks or quarter sections that are assessed in a single assessment;

(iii) any subdivided area that is assessed in a single assessment.

Power of attorney: Legal authority for one to act on behalf of another.

Power of sale: The right of a mortgagee to sell property, secured by mortgage, upon default of the mortgagor. Any mortgagee, provided the mortgage is made by deed, has a power, when the mortgage money becomes due and is not paid by the mortgagor, to sell the mortgaged property.

The proceeds of sale of a mortgage property are used to discharge any prior encumbrance to which the sale is not made subject; to meet the costs of the sale; to pay the mortgagee's debt — principal, interest and costs; to pay the due debts of other mortgagees; and the balance, if any, goes to the mortgagor.

Proceeds: The total amount realized from a public auction or private sale.

Regional municipality: Is a municipality created by a special act of legislature, and is a federation of all the local municipalities within its boundaries. Each of the local municipalities in the region has an elected council, and designated members of all of these councils combine to form the regional council. The regional councils are responsible for regional-scale functions such as overall land-use planning, social services, major roads, and trunk sewer and water systems. Local councils are responsible for community services such as recreation, libraries, local roads and garbage collection.

Reserve Bid (Price): A minimum sale price set prior to public auction.

Right-of-way: The right to pass over another's land more or less freely, according to the nature of the easement.

Road frontage: The distance that a parcel of private property adjoins a public or private road. Substantial road frontage usually greatly enhances the market value of the property.

Second mortgage: A mortgage granted against the security of a property that already has been charged with a first mortgage and, therefore, a mortgage that ranks as a lower priority in the event of any claim against the secured property. A mortgage may be ranked as first, second, third, etc... according to its priority. In practice, any mortgage that is subordinate to a first mortgage may be termed as a second mortgage.

Seizure: The act of taking possession, especially by legal authority or warrant. The act of taking hold or capturing property by force. The forcible taking of possession, in particular by a civil authority or an individual.

Successful purchaser: A successful purchaser is a person whose bid or tender is the highest offered and which is equal to or greater than the cancellation price. The purchaser, as a further condition, must pay the sale price and the land transfer tax with respect to the land and any accumulated real property taxes and interest charges before becoming the successful purchaser.

Survey: Surveyor's report of the mathematical boundaries of land, showing location of buildings, physical features and quantity of land.

Tax arrears: These are real property taxes placed on or added to the collector's roll that remain unpaid on January 1 in the year following that in which they are placed on or added to the roll. For example, taxes levied on January 1, 1991, become arrears if any portion is outstanding on January 1, 1992.

Tax sale: The sale of a property at the instigation of the tax authorities, when the owner of the property has failed to meet a tax liability. The sale is usually by public auction, but it may be arranged by tender or sealed bids. The purchaser may acquire an immediate title (tax title) and possession of the property offered for sale, or his right may be postponed in order to enable the delinquent taxpayer a specified period of time in which to repay the tax. The proceeds of the sale are used to pay the unpaid tax and the balance, if any, is paid to the delinquent tax payer.

In some cases, when tax due on a property remains unpaid, the tax authority may sell, at public auction, a lien they have obtained against the delinquent taxpayer's property. A bidder who pays an amount equal to, or in excess of, the amounts due to the authority acquires a 'tax certificate' which may be converted into ownership of the property if the sums due are not paid by the delinquent taxpayer within a specified redemption period.

Tenancy in common: Ownership of property by two or more persons, whereby on the death of one, his share is credited to his own estate.

Territorial districts: Are divisions of that part of Ontario which does not have county organization. Every district contains a number of local municipalities.

Title: Evidence that the owner of land is in rightful possession of it. Evidence of ownership.

Title deed: Proof of legal ownership of a piece of property.

Title search: Research of the records in a Registry or Land Titles office to determine the history and chain of ownership of the property.

Topography: The accurate and detailed description of land with particular emphasis on surface features and elevations, including hills, valleys, rivers, lakes, roads, etc....

Treasurer: Is the member of the staff whose major duties are to receive and keep all money of the municipality, to issue cheques on behalf of the council, and to prepare the financial statements. Every council is required to appoint a treasurer.

Upset Price: A minimum sale price set prior to public auction.

Unorganized territority: Means, in the strict legal sense, that part of a province without municipal organization.

Vacant land: Is a parcel of land with no buildings on it.

Water rights: The legal privilege granted to one not owning property on which the water facility exists, to use and/or take water for specific purposes that could include fire protection, human consumption, swimming, boating, fishing, and watering of animals.

Water table: The level below which the ground is saturated with water. This is important to know before purchasing a piece of rural property. It is impossible in many areas to have a cellar or basement because of water table conditions. Supply of water from drilled wells is also influenced by water table conditions in the area.

Zoning ordinance: An act of city or county or other authorities specifying the type and use to which property may be put in specified areas.